Legal Forms
For The Designer

Legal Forms
For The Designer

By LEE EPSTEIN

A STANDARD BUSINESS PRACTICE
GUIDE FOR THE DESIGNER

Author's Preface

The legal forms and contracts discussed in this book were originally drafted for the professional society now known as the Industrial Designers Society of America. They have been used by many designers over the years. They have no official connection with that society and, in fact, have been altered in many respects as the result of experience in their use.

Official or not, these forms have met with wide acceptance, not only by designers, but also by manufacturers. During the past few months, one of the largest manufacturers in the country, when he reached an impasse with a designer in negotiating a contract, said, "I'll use the published form of royalty agreement" (meaning the form included in this volume). The existence and repeated acceptance of these legal forms has contributed to a better meeting of the minds between designers and their clients. In effect, they can speak the same language.

A word to lawyers: unlike the forms in most form books, these have not, in general, been subjected to the scrutiny of or interpretation by the courts. This is primarily because most of the clauses are so obvious in meaning that they have not required court interpretation. Most forms that find their way into books of forms have a legal history: They were so ambiguously drawn that their meaning had to be litigated. After a court had interpreted the meaning of a clause, it found its way into a form book, with a footnote citing the case that interprets it. Had it been properly drawn in the first place no interpretation would have been necessary. A simple reading would suffice. For this reason, form books have often been called the burial grounds of poor draftsmanship.

In place of judicial interpretation, on the other hand, the forms included in this manual offer more than 20 years of use undisputed by court litigation as to the meaning of any specific clause. Moreover, the fact that they have been used and accepted by designers and manufacturers for such a long period of time is proof that the clauses are not onerous, but fair and standard practice. This in itself should be persuasive to the prospective clients of designers.

LEE EPSTEIN

Contents

Index of Forms

Page

Part I:
Starting a Business

Methods of Doing Business

The designer who intends to branch out on his own must decide how he wants to do business. He has three choices: he can conduct business as an individual (or a single proprietorship); as a member of a general partnership; or through the medium of a corporation. Each method has certain powers and limitations, benefits or disadvantages as regards taxes and liabilities, and one method may be more suitable than another to the nature of the planned enterprise. The designer should seek the advice and assistance of both an accountant and a lawyer to decide which method best suits his purposes. This chapter explores the advantages and disadvantages of the various methods of doing business and the circumstances to which they apply.

Single Proprietorship

The simplest form of business organization is a single proprietorship. The owner does business either under his own name or under a trade name (such as Atomic Designs). His business and his private affairs are treated as one for the purposes of dealing with creditors; thus his personal assets (car, home, stocks, etc.) are pledged for the purposes of the business and can be reached by his creditors.

Partnership

If two or more individuals combine for the purpose of doing business, the simplest form of organization is a partnership. It may be conducted under a trade name (Atomic Designs, Stratospheric Associates, or the like) or under the names of the partners (Jones, Brown & Smith, or Peabody & Plonck Associates), which must be registered with the local county clerk. This is a joint venture: though the partnership agreement may divide the profits and losses in any proportion between the parties, so far as outsiders are concerned all partners are equally liable for any debts. The private fortune of each partner is available to satisfy the total demands of any creditor of the partnership. Yet, despite their joint responsibilities, partners are taxed as individuals.

A limited partnership (largely unused in design situations) consists of one or more general partners, who are liable to the complete extent of their personal assets, and one or more limited partners, who are liable only to the extent of their contributions to the partnership. For procedural reasons, it is usually more costly to form a limited partnership than a corporation. Limited partnerships are used chiefly for real estate and theatrical ventures because of capital gains tax advantages.

Corporation

A corporation is an entity created under a state statute that lays down certain requirements. These concern, for example: the minimum number of stockholders, usually three to found a corporation (but only one in New York) though later ownership may be concentrated in one person; the number and powers of directors; the calling of stockholders' meetings; the auditing of accounts, and so on. A corporation operates as though it were a person, and can be made perpetual. The stockholders (owners) are liable, except under exceptional circumstances, only for their contribution to the business; the death of a stockholder does not (in the absence of agreement to the contrary) terminate the corporation.

Note on Terminology

The terminology that applies to the different methods of doing business, though it often reflects the powers or limits of that method, is not generally understood. For example, the term "firm" is legally applied only to partnerships. Partners are called "principals" or "partners"; professional (i.e., non-clerical or non-menial) employees who are not partners are usually called "associates." Partners have the power to make commitments and contracts on behalf of the firm (this is explained later in the chapter). Associates do not have this power unless expressly so authorized. A corporation, in most states, must have in its name the word "Incorporated," "Corporation," "Inc.," "Limited," "Ltd.," or similar indication to put prospective creditors on notice that the corporation's liability is limited to its assets. (Some large corporations omit this style from their advertising, either because they were formed before the law required it, or because no creditor could credibly claim to have been misled about the corporate situation.) The word "Company" can be used by an individual, a partnership, or a corporation; but, if used by a corporation, it must be followed by a word denoting incorporation (Inc., Corp., Ltd., etc.).

An individual or a partnership cannot use the name of a person or family in a business name without permission from the person or family—and, in some states, unless the person or member of the family is a partner. And an individual cannot do business under a name denoting plurality (John Jones Associates) unless he is the survivor of a group that did business

4

under that name. A corporation can use any name, provided it is not confusingly similar to another corporate name, or fraudulently used.

The Advantages of Incorporation

For all but the very small or the very new design office, the most advantageous form of organization nowadays is nearly always the corporation. The reasons that in the past discouraged design offices from incorporating have gradually disappeared, as circumstances and the law have altered. The process of forming a corporation is a lot simpler than it sounds, and should not daunt young designers. Below, the advantages of incorporating are explained, and some objections to it discussed.

Immortality and Liability

A corporation is immortal: The death of one or more of the principals does not terminate the business. This makes it more attractive not only for the participants, but also for the client, who knows that the business will continue in spite of death and taxes. A partnership, on the other hand, exists only so long as the partners remain the same; it terminates on death of a partner or other change in its make-up.

The British customarily use the word *Limited* instead of *Incorporated*. This is because a corporation's liability is limited: The principals are liable only for the capital they have invested in the business. This may appear of little value since no great liability seems involved in the average design situation. But large design studios have very large overheads: for instance, annual rent may be, as the banks say, in the high five figures. Such an obligation is easily met when clients are numerous, but it can become difficult if the business falls on hard times. In this event, the corporate form puts the principals' personal fortunes beyond reach of the landlord or other creditors. And, incidentally, the liability of a design studio can, in exceptional cases, be very great.

If a design is so badly conceived that the product becomes dangerous, the designers can be liable for any resulting injury. After the ceiling in the garage of a plush New York apartment house caved in, doing extensive damage to property, the District Attorney called in for examination the architect who had designed the building. In the final event, the architect received a clean bill of health, but the occurrence suggests that it is not impossible for a designer to be held liable in similar circumstances. Of course, it is often possible to carry insurance against such liability; but the corporate form of doing business will limit individuals' liability if the business entity is held for damages beyond the sum insured.

In contrast, a partnership exists only so long as the partners remain the same; it terminates on any change in its make-up or on the death of a partner. And the liability of each partner is unlimited: a creditor can collect his entire claim from any one of the partners even though, as between partners, he may be liable for only a fraction of the firm's debts. (The partner has the right, of course, to collect from his partners the share he has paid to creditors but for which they are liable under the partnership agreement—if they have the money.)

Authority to Make Commitments

Moreover, a partner has apparent authority to make commitments which bind the partnership, despite any limitation agreed upon by the partners (unless the limitation is disclosed); if the partnership is unable to satisfy these commitments, all the partners—including any who did not know of the commitment—may be called upon to do so personally. There is a risk, too, that, if one partner acquires a private liability that he cannot meet (say, damages arising out of an automobile accident not fully covered by insurance) his creditors will reach the other partner's share of the partnership by forcing liquidation of the firm if necessary.

Pensions, Profit-Sharing and Tax

Extensive tax savings are possible to a corporation that are not permitted to a partnership or individual proprietorship. Pension plans and profit-sharing plans offer legitimate shelters against tax liability in the years of greatest earnings. Though the Keogh bill purports to offer some of these advantages to individual proprietors and partners, the limits of that offer are very narrow compared with the benefits available to a corporation. Briefly, a pension plan or a profit-sharing permits a participant to put away, tax free, a substantial part of his earnings, and to accumulate income on that part without paying taxes on it at that time as earned income. Under certain circumstances taxes are payable on the savings and accrued income when received, but these are always lower than they would have been in the years the money was earned. They are usually even lower if they are withdrawn after retirement, when the recipient is no longer in a high tax bracket. More and more design firms have been arranging pension or profit-sharing plans to take advantage of the tax savings—and to provide an incentive for key employees to stay with the firm. This can be done only through a corporation.

The entire tax structure is simpler in a corporation. There is no legal reason why this should be so—it just is so. If an individual designer or a partner uses his automobile for business, and deducts it as a business expense, he usually runs into trouble. The tax examiner insists that the car is used also for pleasure and will allow only a portion of its expenses to be deducted as business expense. On the other hand, if a corporation owns the car and permits an employee to drive it and to charge its expenses to the corporate account, normally the entire expense is allowed to the corporation without fuss. And

7

this is true of many other expenses, when they are paid direct by the corporation and not by way of reimbursement to the employee. The more prosperous a corporation is, the greater the allowance for expenses; the more prosperous an individual is, the more closely his return is examined.

The Objections to Incorporation

The two reasons usually cited against incorporation are: professionalism and, again, taxes. It has often been urged (usually by analogy with doctors and lawyers) that the corporate form is not professional, and therefore designers, particularly industrial designers, who are engaged in a learned profession, should not incorporate. There are several rebuttals to this argument. In the first place, even doctors are now incorporating. In several states, special legislation allows doctors to incorporate for the purpose of taking advantage of the pension plan and profit-sharing privileges available only to corporations: The relationship of a doctor to his patient is still personal, but the fiscal set-up is corporate. Moreover, medicine and the law are not the only learned professions other than design, and in some states the others are permitted (and always have been permitted) to incorporate: engineers and architects, for instance.

Professional Status

The prejudice against incorporation of designers is historical. The New York State Unincorporated Business Tax Act, passed in 1935, placed a compensatory tax on unincorporated businesses to equalize their burden, to some extent, with that of incorporated businesses. To avoid taxing unincorporated enterprises which did not usually use the corporate form, the law excepted "professional activity" from the tax. In the early years of this law, an attempt was made to tax industrial designers under it. Some of the leading designers decided to contest this and, by drawing straws or some such device, the burden fell upon Walter Dorwin Teague. In a suit testing the application of the Unincorporated Business Tax to industrial designers, Teague won a decision that industrial designers were exempt from the tax since they were "professionals."

One result of this decision and the contest leading up to it was the formation of the Society of Industrial Designers (later the American Society of Industrial Designers and now the Industrial Designers' Society of America). The Society, particularly during Mr. Teague's lifetime, was naturally opposed to industrial designers' incorporating, for this would nullify the reasoning of the decision granting them professional status: if industrial designers could incorporate, there was no reason why the unincorporated design office should be exempt from a tax designed to equalize the burden of corporations.

This attitude has gradually been weakened. At first, many design offices operated with two hats: the research, and perhaps the model-making and drafting, were carried on by a corporation, while the design (in the sense of creative work) was done as an individual proprietorship or a partnership. Then the ASID modified its opposition, and opposed incorporation of its members only in those states that did not permit architects or engineers to incorporate. Later, the ASID withdrew all statements of opposition from its by-laws. Many (though not most) IDSA members have now incorporated their businesses; but a number (particularly some of the older, more traditional offices) value what they regard as their professional standing more than the advantages of incorporation.

So far, the New York State tax authorities have not used this trend toward incorporation as ground for challenging the "professional" status of the unincorporated offices—and, with incorporation taking place in some states even among those undoubted professionals, the doctors, they might have a hard time establishing their case.

9

The tax objection to a corporation arose from the fact that a corporation pays taxes on its profits before it distributes them, and then the stockholders pay taxes on the same profits when they receive them as dividends. Here again there are two answers. First, in a closely held corporation like that of the small design groups, there are no dividends since all profits (or almost all) are paid out as salaries and bonuses. Moreover, in 1958 the Federal tax law was amended so that a corporation with ten or fewer stockholders may (in most circumstances) elect to pay taxes as though the corporation did not exist and the stockholders were partners in the enterprise. This gives small corporations the best of both worlds: the advantages of incorporation—limited liability, pension plans, and so on—with freedom from the double taxation that previously discouraged the formation of small corporations.

Beginners—The Small Design Office

In general, the only design office which, perhaps, should not incorporate is the small individual proprietorship or the very small partnership—so small that the few hundred dollars which it costs to incorporate are important, and so small that any liabilities it may incur will be negligible. A small partnership is often the method of association chosen by young designers setting up their own business for the first time. In most states, they must register the name in the county clerk's office for a fee of less than twenty dollars, and can then proceed to earn enough money to grow to a size where incorporation is indicated.

It should be appreciated that a thumbnail sketch of this sort cannot fill in all details. Advice should be sought from local counsel before incorporation is undertaken, and, in some cases, an accountant should be consulted before the exact form the corporation should take (amount of stock, classification of shares, and so on) is determined.

10

Papers to be Filed at the Formation of Business

Individual Proprietorship and Partnerships

If a designer is going to do business as an individual under his own simple name, he need file no papers with state or local authorities in order to do so. What he must do if he plans to hire employees, however, is secure an employer's number for tax and social security purposes regardless of the nature of his business. Application forms for these numbers can be obtained from any post office. In states like New York that have sales tax laws, the designer will also need a resale number. Application forms for these can be obtained from the tax collecting authority.

If the designer plans to do business under a name other than his own simple name—even if his name is John Jones and he will call his business the John Jones Company or John Jones Design—he must file a certificate with the County Clerk (in New York) or appropriate authority in other states. The purpose of the "doing business as" certificate is to enable anyone to learn by examining the clerk's records just who comprises the John Jones Company or John Jones Design. This becomes necessary in cases of advancing credit to the new company and, of course, in the case of a law suit. When the form is filed, the applicant can obtain a certified copy of the certificate for a small fee (usually one dollar). By showing the certified copy to his bank, he can cash or deposit checks made out to John Jones Company. Without such proof, the bank will be unwilling to open an account or to cash or collect checks made out in the company name.

When two or more designers will do business as partners, they must file a business certificate that is similar in form to

11

the one for individual proprietorship. Again, this merely puts on record with the local authorities who the partners are and the certificate is filed for the reasons just given.

Examples of business certificates for individuals and for partnerships follow at the end of this chapter.

The actual agreement between the partners themselves need not be filed. The ramifications and possible variations in a partnership agreement are so varied that there is no one form that could serve to illustrate a "typical" agreement. A lawyer should be consulted to draw up the terms agreed upon between the partners.

Incorporation

Incorporation, though it may sound like a complicated legal process, is really quite a simple matter. The designers who wish to form a corporation must consult a lawyer to advise them on filing procedures and write-up of the papers of incorporation. The going rate for incorporation in New York is roughly $250, which generally includes the costs of filing papers with the state authorities plus a mark-up for legal counsel.

Legal counsel for the new corporation will extend to clearing the corporate name, wording of the documents, filing of papers, issuance of stock, and rough assessment of their value. It can often include advice on the most suitable way of handling taxes for the individuals and other intra-corporate matters.

Because the papers of incorporation are secured from, granted by and filed with the state authorities, this eliminates the need to file the "doing business as" certificate. The new corporation must obtain the employer's number in order to hire employees other than the officers of the corporation, and a resale number if the state in which the corporation is organized has sales tax laws. The method of obtaining these numbers is the same as listed for individual proprietorship and partnerships.

A general form for the Certificate of Incorporation, based on the laws of New York State, is included at the end of the chapter. It should be noted that in some states, New York for one, the Office of the Secretary of State is wary of including "designing" among the corporate powers, lest the term be construed to include engineering or architectural services. Neither of the latter powers is permitted to corporations organized in New York State. A charter readily passes, however, if the papers contain a subclause that expressly excludes engineering and architecture from the corporate powers. This subclause appears in the sample form.

Business Certificate

I HEREBY CERTIFY that I am conducting or transacting business under the name or designation of

JOHN JONES DESIGNS

at   *123 Fifth Avenue*

City or Town of   *New York*   County of   *New York* State of New York.

My full name is   *JOHN JONES*

and I reside at   *456 Jones Street, New York, N. Y. 10001*

[If under 21 years of age, state age]

IN WITNESS WHEREOF, I have this   *3RD*   day of *October*   1968, made and signed this certificate.

S/ *John Jones*

Business Certificate for Partners

The undersigned do hereby certify that they are conducting or transacting business as members of a partnership under the name or designation of

JONES & BROWN DESIGN ASSOCIATES

at   *123 Fifth Avenue, New York City*

in the County of   *New York*   , State of New York, and do further certify that the full names of all the persons conducting or transacting such partnership including the full names of all the partners with the residence address of each such person, and the age of any who may be infants, are as follows:

NAME (Specify which are infants and state ages.)

John Jones

Tom Brown

RESIDENCE

456 Jane Street, New York, N.Y. 10001

789 Horatio Street, New York, N.Y. 10001

IN WITNESS WHEREOF, We have this   *30th*   day of   *October*   *1968*   made and signed this certificate.

S/ John Jones

S/ Tom Brown

15

Form: Certificate of Incorporation

CERTIFICATE OF INCORPORATION

– of –

UNIVERSAL DESIGNERS, Inc.

Under Section 402 of the Business Corporation **Law**

The undersigned, being a natural person of at least 21 years of age and acting as the incorporator of the Corporation, hereby being formed under the Business Corporation Law of the State of New York, certifies:

FIRST: The name of the Corporation shall be
UNIVERSAL DESIGNERS, Inc.

SECOND: The Corporation is formed for the following purposes:

To engage in the business of interior, industrial and graphic design, to buy and sell products of all sorts and to engage in the business of space planning, but nothing contained herein shall permit the corporation to engage in the business or professions of engineering or architecture.

To engage in a general merchandising and manufacturing business, and to purchase, manufacture or otherwise acquire, pledge, lease, invest in, make or receive consignments or bailments of, import, export, mortgage, sell, assign and transfer, or otherwise dispose of, and generally to deal in commodities and products and merchandise, goods, wares, machinery, fabrics of every description, whether natural or synthetic, printed materials, and articles of commerce, whether constituting real or personal property, of every kind, character and description whatsoever, and wheresoever situated, at any place or places in the United States of America or foreign countries throughout the world.

To act as broker, or as commercial, sales, business commission merchant, or financial agent, factor del credere or otherwise, or as attorney-in-fact for individuals, co-partnerships, joint stock associations or corporations, foreign or domestic, including governments or governmental authorities; and to aid and assist, promote and conserve the interests of and afford facilities for the continuous transaction of business by its principals and patrons in the United States of America or in foreign countries throughout the world.

To act as forwarding, shipping and freight agent and as clearance and customhouse broker.

To purchase or otherwise hold, own, maintain, improve, operate, mortgage, sell, convey or otherwise dispose of, and to lease real and personal property of every class and description in any of the states, districts or territories of the United States and in any foreign countries, subject to the laws of such state, district, territory or country.

To purchase or otherwise acquire, hold, use, sell, assign, lease, grant licenses in respect of, mortgage or otherwise dispose of letters patent of the United States or any foreign country, patent rights, licenses and privileges, inventions, improvements and processes, copyrights, trademarks and trade names.

For its purposes, on any terms and without limit, to borrow or receive money, and, from time to time, to make, accept, endorse, execute and issue bonds, debentures, promissory notes, drafts, bills of exchange and other obligations of the corporation, and to secure the payment of any such obligations by mortgage, pledge, deed, indenture, agreement or other instruments of trust, or by other lien upon, assignment of or agreement in regard to all or any part of the property rights or privileges of the corporation wherever situated, whether now owned or hereafter to be acquired.

To purchase or otherwise acquire, hold, cancel, reissue, sell, resell, pledge, transfer and otherwise dispose of its own shares, so far as may be permitted by law.

To purchase, hold, sell, assign, transfer, mortgage, pledge or otherwise dispose of shares of capital stock of, or bonds, securities, or evidences of indebtedness created by any other corpora-

17

tion or corporations organized under the law of this state or any other state, country, nation or government, and while the owner thereof, to exercise all the rights, powers, and privileges of ownership.

To make, enter into, perform and carry out contracts, agreements, and obligations of every sort and kind, which may be necessary or convenient for the business of this company or business of a similar nature, with any person, firm, corporation, private, public or municipal, body politic under the government of the United States or any state, territory, possession or colony thereof, or any foreign government, so far as, and to the extent that, the same may be done and performed by corporations organized under the New York Business Corporation Law.

To acquire and pay for in cash, shares or bonds of this corporation or otherwise, the good will, rights, assets and property, and to undertake or assume the whole or any part of the obligations or liabilities of any person, firm, association or corporation.

To do all and everything necessary or convenient for the accomplishment of the objects or purposes herein enumerated, or necessary, incidental or appropriate to the protection of the corporation.

In general, to carry on any other similar business in connection with the foregoing, and to have and exercise all the powers conferred from time to time by the laws of New York upon corporations formed under the New York Business Corporation Law and to do any or all of the things hereinbefore set forth to the same extent as natural persons might or could do.

The foregoing clauses of this ARTICLE SECOND shall be construed as purposes, objects and powers, and the matters expressed in each clause shall not be limited in any way, except as otherwise expressly provided, by reference to or inference from the terms of any other clause (or any other matter within the same clause), but shall be regarded as independent purposes, objects and powers; and the enumeration of specified purposes, objects and powers shall not be construed to exclude, limit or restrict in any manner any power, right or privilege given to the corporation by law, or to limit or restrict in any manner the meaning of the general terms of such clauses, or the general powers of the corporation, nor shall the expression of one thing be deemed to exclude another, although it be of like nature, not expressed.

THIRD: The city, incorporated village or town and the county within the State of New York in which the office of the corporation is to be located are as follows:

City, Incorporated Village or Town	County
New York City	*New York*

FOURTH: The aggregate number of shares which the corporation shall have authority to issue is *200* shares, *all of which shall be without* Par Value, all of which are of the same class and all of which are designated as common shares.

FIFTH: The Secretary of State is designated as the agent of the corporation upon whom process in any action or proceeding against the corporation may be served. The post office address to which the Secretary of State shall mail a copy of any process against the corporation served upon him is:

℅ John Brown, 456 Jane Street, New York, N.Y. 10001

SIXTH: Except as may otherwise be specifically provided in this certificate of incorporation, no provision of this certificate of incorporation is intended by the corporation to be construed as limiting, prohibiting, denying, or abrogating any of the general or specific powers or rights conferred under the Business Corporation Law upon the corporation, upon its shareholders, bondholders, and security holders, and upon its directors, officers, and other corporate personnel, including, in particular, the power of the corporation to furnish indemnification to directors and officers in the capacities defined and prescribed by the Business Corporation Law and the defined and prescribed rights of said persons to indemnification as the same are conferred by the Business Corporation Law.

IN WITNESS WHEREOF, the undersigned has executed and acknowledged this certificate this *31st* day of *October,* nineteen hundred and sixty-*eight.*

S/ John Jones
_____
(Incorporator)

456 Jane Street
New York, N.Y. 10001
_____
(Address of Incorporator)

Part II:
The Nature of Contracts

Are Contracts Necessary?

There are designers who believe that they can conduct business, engage clients and execute projects, without any agreement, formal or informal. Some of these designers have never had any difficulty collecting fees for their services. Others have not been so lucky. Some found when they consulted lawyers in the face of difficulties that they did indeed have binding agreements—or contracts—though these were harder to prove because of their ambiguous business approach. The less fortunate designers found they didn't have a leg to stand on, legally, and could not recover their fees.

At the outset of a business relationship, the question arises: Do we need a contract at all? Potential clients often say: "I believe that if you're dealing with an honest person, you can do business on a handshake," or "Contracts are made to be broken," or "Anyone who wants to get out of a contract can do it." They may even say that asking a lawyer whether you need a contract is like asking a surgeon whether or not you need an operation.

There are several answers to these gambits. In the first place, willingness to enter into an agreement is a sign of good faith.

If a person intends to live up to his undertakings, there is no reason in the world why he should not be willing to state what these undertakings are. An honest man is not afraid to "put it in writing." Beware the man who insists that he won't commit himself as a "matter of honor." Let him put his pen where his mouth is.

The second reason: a contract, by specifying the obligations of each party, avoids future misunderstandings. Thus, disagreements about whether the designer must supply rough sketches or working drawings, dates on which various stages of the work are to be completed, time and method of payment, who pays certain development costs, etc., will not take place if the parties have discussed these matters and reached (and written) agreement on them.

On more than one occasion, a client has asked me to draw up a contract for a project on which he thought he was in full agreement with his client. When I pressed him for details, it became evident that the parties had not yet really agreed—in fact, had not even considered many details that should be firm before performance is begun. The very act of discussing the details helps the parties to clarify their positions.

Another case for written contracts is a strong one. Certain contracts, by law referred to as "The Statute of Frauds," are unenforceable unless they are in writing. This is the law's rather cynical recognition of the fact that, if oral evidence is received in these cases, fraud may creep in. Both parties are therefore cautioned to secure a written record of their agreement, on pain of not being able to enforce it otherwise.

Furthermore, while a designer may (perhaps improvidently) have the utmost faith in the client with whom he is dealing, he may not be dealing with the same person by the time the project nears completion.

The person with whom the deal was made may die. The designer then finds himself dealing with an executor or heir.

If it is an executor, he will usually say, "I am responsible to the court and the heirs and cannot disburse any money unless I have written proof that it is due. Even if I believe personally that the money is due, I cannot support the payment in an accounting and thus my hands are tied."

I know of several instances in which widows refused to carry through deals made by their late husbands, giving the argument, "He never told me about it and I can find nothing in his business records to that effect." The laws of many states uphold the reasoning behind this position by forbidding anyone who asserts a claim against an estate from testifying about his transaction with the deceased. Any testimony regarding the transaction must come from a third party. The reasoning here is: it would be easy to claim anything when the man with whom the deal was made is not present to confirm or deny it.

In another instance, the person with whom the designer originally dealt may have resigned or been discharged. The designer must then deal with a successor, who may want to challenge the deal made by his predecessor, or he may appeal (like the executor) to his duty to those widows and orphans, the stockholders.

Then, too, the client may merge with or be acquired by another corporation. This danger is significant in the present heyday of the conglomerate corporation. In recent years, designers who dealt with Documat found themselves working for International Tel & Tel; those who dealt with Creative Playthings found that they were working for Columbia Broadcasting (this also applies to baseball players who were working for the New York Yankees); designers who made agreements with Lehigh Furniture ended up with Litton Industries, and those who originally dealt with Knoll found themselves first with Art Metal and later with Heller. In the cases named, management was usually retained and the designer was not affected by the change. In others (who shall remain nameless),

24

the new management brought in a staff of sharp-eyed graduates of Harvard Business School who specialized in finding ways out of situations they considered unprofitable. They could (and did) make difficulties for designers who asserted rights that they could not prove in writing.

For these and many other reasons, such as transfer, promotion, or the like, the designer may have no one to look to for the faithful fulfillment of his expectations if there is no written contract.

When a prospective client suggests that a designer have faith in him instead of demanding a contract, it is not always easy to insist on one. But few people will resent the statement, "That would be all right if we knew we'd both be here forever. Suppose one of us is hit by a taxi next week? Aren't you entitled to have some protection from a claim by my wife that I was to get not five but ten thousand dollars? And am I not entitled to some evidence to show your executor or successor what our agreement actually was?"

A contract is not devised to be the basis for a law suit—it is, rather, designed to avoid law suits by defining the obligations of both sides so clearly that they are obvious to all parties and litigation is unnecessary.

But it is the possibility of litigation that keeps the morally marginal man honest. While it is true that "any contract made can be broken," it cannot be broken with impunity. As long as the rule of law prevails, the person whose contract rights are denied has the right to recover damages. Court records are replete with judgments against people who thought that "contracts were made to be broken."

What Constitutes a Contract?

Without going into such legal requirements as consideration (which is not relevant to this discussion, since all of the contracts considered are supported by consideration on both sides), mutuality and the differences between bilateral and unilateral obligations, it is sufficient for us to consider as a contract any arrangement for work to be done or goods to be sold marked by what old-fashioned lawyers call a "meeting of the minds" and more modern ones call "mutual manifestations of assent." In plain talk, if both parties indicate that they are agreed, that's a contract.

In old Roman days, one party to a contract would sometimes ask "Spondes" (are you agreed?) and the other would reply "Spondeo" (I agree!). They would strike hands, and they had a contract. This was the old way, and required a formality (the striking of hands) before witnesses and an intention to make a contract.

Until the formal ritual had been carried out, no binding arrangement was reached. A man could say, "I'll give you thirty talents of silver for your cow," but you couldn't hold him to it until you both had "struck hands" before witnesses.

It was, incidentally, from this striking of the hands that the phrase "striking a bargain" arose, as did the still prevalent custom of shaking hands to seal a bet or other bargain.

Nowadays, no such formality is required. No specific words are needed—in fact, no words are needed at all. If a person is walking to the train and passes the grocer, he may pick up an apple, wave it at the grocer, who waves back. At the end of the month, when his bill arrives, it includes: 1 apple, 10¢. His silent wave and the grocer's equally silent answering wave constituted a contract—they were mutual manifestations of assent to the transaction—the sale of one apple.

But I am not suggesting that this is the sort of contract designers should make. For one thing, as mentioned earlier, there are some contracts that must, as a matter of law, be in writing lest they be barred by the Statute of Frauds. Further, as an old saw of lawyers goes: "The strongest promise is weaker than the palest ink," or, as Sam Goldwyn put it, "An oral promise isn't worth the paper it's written on." Finally, the attempt to prove an oral contract often shows merely that the parties never agreed to the same thing. A strong reason for a contract is that it lets each party know what his obligations are; an oral understanding is often a misunderstanding. The act of putting it in writing makes each item clearer and avoids ambiguity and possible future conflict.

Although an agreement should be in writing, it need not have a particular form. Some lawyers prefer a form which begins:

THIS AGREEMENT, made in the City and State of New York by and between JOHN DOE, of 123 Broadway in the City and State of New York, hereinafter referred to as Party of the First Part, and RICHARD ROE, of 456 Fifth Avenue, in the City and State of New York, hereinafter referred to as Party of the Second Part, WITNESSETH;

WHEREAS, the Party of the first part, etc., etc.

There is nothing wrong with this form. In fact, it has for

a lazy person, certain advantages: it supplies a ready-made skeleton that is simple to flesh out; it has the magic of an incantation that makes the client feel he is getting a legal document; on the other hand, it is often so abstruse that the client must refer to a lawyer whenever he wants to learn the meaning of any clause. A full discussion of the various forms that contracts may take is the subject of the next chapter.

Negotiating the Contract

Upon signing a contract recently, a manufacturer confided to me, "That's the best contract I ever gave a designer." I replied, "But that's not the best you're going to give." What did I mean? Negotiating a series of contracts is like courting a girl. On each date you start where you left off the last time. New contracts also "start with the last one" and the main objective each time is to negotiate the improvements. Anyone who has had experience negotiating labor agreements knows the truth of this statement.

The tactics involved in negotiating a contract can improve its terms for the designer. Knowing what to be wary of, knowing what terms to reject, laying the groundwork for better terms in the future are all a part of negotiating the satisfactory agreement. Say, for instance, that a prospective client suggests a modest fee (or royalty) with the proviso that if the designs are successful, the compensation will be increased at a later date. On the surface, the suggestion is perfectly reasonable— but it should be rejected nevertheless. Why?

Once the agreement is signed at a certain rate, the designer becomes labelled in the mind of his client as one who can be talked into a lower rate. Unless the designs are wildly successful, the designer may find it extremely difficult to inch the client up from the original price.

The difficulty could have been minimized at the outset by artful negotiations. The client could have been persuaded to insert a clause in the original contract stating that the rate will be increased at a future date, or better still, specifying the new rate. The client may not honor the clause, since it is really nothing more than an agreement to make another agreement. There is nothing to prevent him from countering, "I can give you the new contract but unfortunately we cannot afford the higher rate." Nevertheless, the clause does imply a certain moral obligation on the part of the client that may prick his conscience at the time the new contract is being negotiated.

Contracts can often be improved in ways other than monetary: by requiring the use of the designer's name; by setting time limits within which the designs must be produced and returned; by increasing the advance (which will not usually change the net take from the contract, but will encourage the client to sell the designs earlier and more vigorously, etc.).

Another way to improve the terms of a contract is through the use of an agent. I am all for them—if a good one can be found. How can a designer boast about himself or give a good hard sell without running the risk that the prospective client think him pompous or a braggart? But an agent can praise the designer and his talents, and, in fact, it is his role to do so. A good agent can often get a designer better terms than he can get for himself.

But a good agent is hard to find. He will want a drawing account against commissions and, since design jobs take many months to sell, the designer may find that he has paid a draw for six months with nothing to show for it. He may not know whether he will ever have anything to show for it. The obvious solution is to employ an agent (like an actor's agent) on commission only. Unfortunately, I have never found one worth his salt who was willing to work without a draw.

What Should the
Contract Provide?

The ideal contract is one that is so complete that the parties look at it, sign it and put it in the file, where it rests undisturbed. The contract should set forth and define the exact limits or commitments of the parties involved. At a minimum, it would provide a description of the job, when and in what form it will be delivered, and at what fee.

In complex projects or those involving a client/manufacturer in a highly competitive industry or a well-known designer, the contract may include provisos for the use of the designer's name and the context in which it will be allowed; exclusivity, or a restriction of the designer to work in competing areas of the same industry. It may also provide for royalties on product design, and even patents, especially in industrial design projects where the development of new products is a natural consequence of solving the problem.

This chapter explores, in general, the provisos of the standard contract. Because of the complexity of fees, royalties and patents, the latter are touched upon briefly here but discussed in full in later chapters.

Times of Performance

The client often wants to set a deadline for complete performance on the part of the designer—to meet the date of a trade show, a market opening or the like. There is no objection to doing this if it is made clear that meeting the deadline is contingent on the client's cooperation. Often a designer will submit preliminary sketches, and the client will sit on them— until his sales manager is back in town, or his wife returns from vacation, or each of his sales representatives throughout the country has had a chance to pass judgment on them. Then, after many months, the designs are returned to the designer a week before the deadline for finished drawings, leaving insufficient time for even the fastest worker to meet the date established. This makes it look as though the designer is at fault, although the failure to meet the deadline is due to failure of the client to cooperate. It may also create havoc in the designer's studio, because he may have set aside certain time and facilities for completion of the designs. The delay may require (at the best) overtime that was not considered when the rate for the job was established.

It is simple and inoffensive to provide in the agreement that if all preliminary work is returned within ten days of submission, the final drawing will be submitted by such a date or, even better, that the final drawing will be submitted within so many days of the return of the preliminary drawing with approvals.

Statement of Fees

When fixing the fee for design services, the parties should be sure that they both know what the fee covers. Besides outlining the work to be done by the designer, the agreement

31

should indicate whether the fee covers model making, detail drawings, elaborate renderings, any design services which may be bought outside of the designer's office (such as typography, graphics on certain jobs, etc.), extra copies of blue prints and plans, messenger service, long distance telephone calls, and the like. Normally, all of the aforementioned items, plus the cost of travel and expenses while traveling, are billed separately in addition to the design fee. In order to protect the client, the agreement usually provides that expenses in excess of a specific amount, say $25, will be subject to the approval of the client. This does not require *prior* approval, but it does place any expenses incurred without prior approval at the risk of the designer, since if such approval is not secured, he will not be reimbursed for them.

Reimbursement for expenses may seem a trivial matter, but expenses can run into large sums on some projects. It is not unheard of for a client to suggest, for example, that trips to his plant should be at the designer's expense, when there has been no prior discussion of this detail.

Exclusivity

The client will often insist that the designer agree that, for the term of his employment, he will not perform any design services for anyone engaged in a business similar to that of the client. This is not an unreasonable condition under the proper circumstances. If the designer is being adequately compensated for the exclusivity, he should give it. However, this is not the same thing as being adequately compensated for the job. A design job worth $1,000, commanding a fee of $1,000, does not justify requiring the designer to agree to eliminate himself from a field in which he might normally earn $10,000. Either exclusivity must be expressly paid for or it must result from the contract price being sufficiently high to warrant the designer's consent to cut off other sources of income.

The area of exclusivity should be carefully considered. It should be broad enough to give the client adequate protection from having to compete with other designs of the designer, but it should not be broader than necessary to accomplish that purpose. For example, if the client is a manufacturer of earthenware dishes, he is not really in competition with higher priced vitreous ware, and it is not reasonable to expect the designer to grant exclusivity in the entire dinnerware field.

A troublesome question arises when the client is one of those octopus companies with interests in many fields. Instead of granting such a client the exclusive right to the designer's services in *all* of these fields, it is customary to give the client the right of refusal in the field other than those in which the designer has agreed to submit designs. This means that if the designer wants to act in these other fields, he must give the client first call on his services. Such an arrangement has the double advantage of giving the client as broad protection as he wants to exercise, without cutting the designer off from further opportunities. This type of clause often leads to the designer working in increasingly broad areas for the same client.

Use of Name

It is often difficult to get a manufacturer to agree to use the designer's name on a product, or a job, but the effort should always be made. The better-known designers did not become well known by hiding their lights under bushel baskets. Their reputations grew through emphasis and insistence on the use of their names until they are now able to offer a trade name as well as design services. Particularly in the field of consumer products, the designer should initiate a regular program of having his name used wherever possible.

Of course, as the designer's name becomes well known, resistance to its use diminishes, until (as mentioned above) it

33

becomes a desirable by-product of the design contract.

Whenever the use of the designer's name is licensed, or required, it should be conditional on the maintenance of the quality of the product. The usual procedure is for the designer to approve standard samples or prototypes and to permit (or require) his name to be used as long as the merchandise produced meets the specifications of the standard. If it falls below, the designer's name must be removed until the quality has been restored to standard. Such a clause prevents the designer's name from being cheapened by association with shoddy merchandise, and the designer's insistence on the integrity of his name increases the client's respect for it and may become a decisive factor in the client's decision to use it.

The minimum that a designer should require is that his name be used in publicity releases to the trade and that he be permitted to make fair use of the pictures and description of the product in his own promotion pieces. A designer's business usually expands like ripples from a pebble dropped in water; the best sources of business are firms in the same general field as those already served. If a designer's name is not a household word, at least he can hope that it appears in the trade journals, so that when he makes a pitch for new business and says, "I'm the fellow who designed the 'so-and-so' lamp," the prospect will at least say, "Now I know why your name was familiar. I saw it in the publicity in the *Lamp Journal.*"

Patents

Many designs created by industrial designers are not qualified for valid patent protection. However, if they do qualify for such protection, the designer customarily agrees to assign his rights in the designs to the client. A preferable arrangement is one whereby the designer agrees to execute an exclusive license to the client in his field. Thus, if a designer evolves a new method of suspension for a filing cabinet drawer, and his client makes only filing cabinets, the designer may be able to use the same invention for desk drawers for another client, or for medicine cabinets, or food lockers, or refrigerators. Here again, the license given to the client should be only as broad as is necessary to give the client a completely exclusive license in his field, without giving him a free ride by permitting him to license non-competitors in other fields. This should be the privilege of the designer. Some designers of fabric have licensed the use of their designs for wallpapers, or even for dishes, without limiting the utilization of the designs to their immediate client. In some cases, this has benefited the client, since the associated designs sell better when they are marketed as part of an ensemble which would not have been within the power of the first client to assemble.

Particularly in royalty contracts, the license of the rights in the designs is preferable to a patent assignment. It gives the client all of the rights he needs, but in case of breach of contract by the client, or his insolvency, or his discontinuance of a design, it is much simpler to license another client than to go through the difficult procedure of obtaining a reassignment of the patent.

There is an additional advantage in making the contract a license to use a patent rather than the sale of services or the right to use an unpatented design. The Revenue Act treats income from the license of a patent as *capital gains income* rather than as regular income. It is, therefore, taxed at capital gains rates which are never more than half of regular tax rates and may be lower. The designer who has such a contract finds himself ranged alongside of the oil millionaire in receiving favorable tax treatment. Care should be exercised in drawing a licensing agreement if this tax advantage is desired, and the advice of a lawyer should be sought.

What Form Should
Contracts Take?

There is no magic rule that will, when applied to a sheet of paper, make a good contract. Various forms are adapted to different purposes and can be used with different clients.

The forms suggested in this book represent an ideal situation. They are normative, rather than descriptive of the usual contract. It may often be necessary to change the forms in order to make them acceptable to a prospective client. Whether or not a specific change requested should be agreed to is a business decision to be made by the designer. The classic recipe for rabbit stew begins, "First catch your rabbit." * In order to enter into a contract with a client, he must first agree to its terms. But it does not necessarily follow that any concessions demanded must be granted. The designer's willingness to change a form is, as mathematicians say, a function of his interest in the proposed job, his need for work, his estimate

---

* This phrase appears in the classic American cook book. One of the European recipes begins, "Steal a rabbit."

of the concessions other reputable designers might be willing to make in order to get the job, and his estimate of the client's interest in his ability.

Printed vs. Typewritten Contracts

There are occasions on which the long form contract (perhaps in a simpler, more elegant form than the model quoted on page 52) is indicated. As will appear from the discussion below, certain arrangements, particularly royalty agreements, are often complex enough to warrant a full fledged lawyer-type contract (these are explained in full later in the book). But when such a contract is submitted, I suggest that it be printed.

Why a printed contract? There is something about a printed document that inhibits amendment. It seems to say, "This is our policy." Of course, an apt rejoinder is, "Then change your policy," but this suggestion is rarely made. The most one-sided legal document that the average person sees in his lifetime is a lease; it is completely lopsided, and usually contains clauses that are not only unfair, but also actually unenforceable because they are contrary to the law. Yet, most tenants sign them as submitted even in the days before rent control or the landlord's market prevailed.

On the other hand, when a designer tenders a typewritten contract, his client feels that he must submit it to his lawyer. The lawyer usually suggests changes, in even the fairest agreement—perhaps to prove that he has read it, or perhaps to justify a fee—in any case, out of a feeling that he must gain for his client some little advantage before the agreement is executed. Thus, a typewritten agreement is an invitation to amendment, *but a printed agreement seems sacrosanct.*

Another reason why a printed contract may be advisable is that it establishes the conditions under which the designer works. One of the members of the American Society of Industrial Designers has had forms (based on the Society's suggested standards) printed and, at the first business interview with a prospective client, gives him a blank form, saying, "This will give you an idea of how we work." By the time a decision to retain the designer is reached (if one is reached) the client has already absorbed and probably agreed to most of the terms, leaving only a few sections and the blanks (like payment, dates of delivery of designs, etc.) to be negotiated.

Formal Document vs. The Informal Letter of Agreement

However, a contract need not be in legalese. It can consist of a simple letter, agreed to by the addressee.

It is not enough, though, merely to write a letter; the letter must be acknowledged by the recipient and agreed to. It takes two not only to tango, but also to make a contract. Many designers who have written letters to their clients, summarizing their agreements, have been unable to prove, without some writing from their client, that an agreement was reached. A letter is a self-serving document; it needs something from the recipient to make it binding. While recent changes in the law may, in some instances, bind the client if he fails to contradict what the letter says, it is safer and more certain to ask for an acknowledgment of the letter and its terms. This is done by including a carbon copy, on which is typed such a phrase as "Agreed to" or "I (or we) agree to the foregoing," followed by the client's name and a line for the signature of the person agreeing for the client. The client is then asked to sign and return the carbon copy if the terms are satisfactory.

Whether a short form letter or a long "legalese" contract is offered, make sure that the document or the letter tendering the document looks like a designer's message. It is surprising how often designers who command fees of thousands of dollars for helping a client project a proper corporate image, have no regard for their own identity as designers.

At Harvard Law School, when a student stammers or

flounders in a recitation, the professors say, "Sir, try to make noises like a lawyer!" Similarly, when a designer communicates with a client or a prospective client, he should try to "make noises like" a designer.

The letterhead on which a letter is written, the envelope in which it is enclosed, the spelling and the very arrangement of the typing contribute to the client's impression of the designer. Every contract or proposal tendered is not only a legal document, it is also a sales instrument—a part of your attempt to get the client to sign on the dotted line. If your letterhead is clumsy, or the letter misspelled, the client will (either consciously or subconsciously) say, "What kind of designer is this; he can't even see how badly his own letterhead is designed."

I have frequently had trouble with design students who didn't know how to spell. Their response to criticism often is "We don't have to know how to spell—we're designers (or artists)." This is a serious mistake. Designers correspond with client's employees at the highest echelons. These are not illiterate workers who have won promotion by use of their brawn, but are usually cultivated, literate, highly articulate men who can spot (and wince at) a misspelling at fifty paces.

If a designer is not a graphics specialist, he can hire one; if he is not a good speller, he can check with a dictionary. At the outset, the first investment a designer should make, and one on which he should not scrimp, is a good business card and stationery of good quality.

So far as literary style is concerned, the only thing that the designer need worry about is simplicity. An old English teacher's adage goes: Write not to be understood, but to avoid all possibility of being misunderstood. This should be amended to read: Write not merely to be understood, but to be understood clearly and simply.

Many young designers feel that if they can fill a letter with circumlocutions and high-flown phraseology, they will give their correspondence a big business look. This just makes a letter difficult to read. Your audience consists of busy men; if they have to extract the meaning from your letter like the meat from a lobster claw, they are not going to take the time. Your letter will go into the "file" basket.

The Value of Enthusiasm

On the other hand, the remedy for verbosity is not complete informality. You are writing to a business acquaintance, not a fraternity brother. Your style can be clear and simple without back-slapping. A mix of enthusiasm, competence and respect is probably ideal. Respect does not mean fawning servility, but it never hurts to err on the side of formality. The prep school boys who have learned the proper use of the title "Sir" have never suffered by it.

The ability to convey a sense of your enthusiasm for the job is essential. For example, the score sheets that one of the government agencies uses in rating bids for design work scores on a scale of 100. Price (as long as it is within the budget limits) counts for only 5 points. But "enthusiasm and interest in the job" counts for 25 points. Thus, a designer whose price is higher than another designer's may nevertheless get the job if he seems to be more enthusiastic and more interested in the job.

How is this enthusiasm conveyed? Everyone must use his own style. No one can write a complete letter which expresses another's personality. But one good way to show enthusiasm is by frankly saying it: "I am deeply interested in doing this job and have been considering various approaches to the problem involved. I would like to work with your engineering group on this project." This can, of course, be stated in many ways and altered to meet the needs of the situation, but this attitude should always be considered and should usually be expressed. The client is chiefly interested in what you are going to do for him and is appealed to by the fact that you are excited by the project. It may be very difficult for you to work up enthusiasm over the redesign of his pickle fork, but if you can't (or at least if you can't convince him that you are enthusiastic) you won't get the job, and probably shouldn't.

This brings up the matter of the finale of the letter. Writers of sales letters are careful to finish them with some language calculated to get the recipient to "do it now!" This may be a special offer of a premium or price if the letter is answered within a certain number of days. It may be a recapitulation of what the writer thinks are the strongest selling points. In any case, it consists of language that, it is hoped, will overcome the normal tendency to set the letter aside on a corner of the desk where it languishes until it is forgotten.

I often remind my students of the "Dixie finish" which was once popular in vaudeville. At the end of an act—very often a dull act—the actor would slip an American flag out of his pocket and wave it over his head; the band would strike up "The Stars and Stripes Forever" and the actor would dance off the stage to thunderous applause. A "Dixie finish" is useful in a designer's letter. If the designer can convey some feeling of excitement or enthusiasm in the closing lines of his letter, he is much more likely to get the client to sign on the dotted line. Too many letter proposals end, like T.S. Eliot's world, not with a bang but with a whimper.

Stating the Fee

The amount of your fee is determined by many factors discussed in a later chapter, but its placement in your letter or proposal is pertinent. For many years I have had students write proposals (usually in letter form) as part of their classroom exercises. Despite frequent and repeated admonitions against the practice, most of the letters begin: "Dear Mr. Jones: This is a proposal for the redesign of your pickle fork. For a fee of

41

$———, I will undertake the job——" This is the worst way to make the proposal. It hits the client first with the cost (which is the chief factor in building up sales resistance) instead of emphasizing what he will get. If the letter is properly drawn, it will set forth the designer's work in such detail and at such length that by the time the price is quoted it will seem miniscule for the job.

This doesn't mean that the designer must flinch at quoting a price. A designer is a member of a skilled and respected profession. He is entitled to a fair price for his work, commensurate with the importance of the job, his skill and the time involved. At the proper place, set forth the price, and the manner of payment. "My fee will be $10,000, payable in ten monthly installments of $1,000 each, commencing September 1st." This leaves no doubt either about the price for the job or about the manner of payment. Avoid a technique which seems to shun quoting the price. Some business advisory firms sell their services by quoting the price for an annual service as "$4 per month, the annual cost payable after receipt of the first pamphlet." What they mean is that their charge is $48, which amounts to only $4 per month on a yearly basis. But they are afraid that the $48 figure will scare off potential customers. I have always been repelled by this technique and suggest that a designer should treat his clients more candidly and give them credit for being able to multiply the monthly payments by the number of months. The only fee which should be quoted in dollars per month is a monthly retainer because it is logical to quote this way.

Part III:
Fees and Fee Structures

How Are Designers Paid?

Both designers and manufacturers frequently ask what is the fair method and rate of payment for design service. This chapter reviews the methods most often employed: the flat fee, the straight-time arrangement, retainers, and consultation fees. It also outlines the agreements drawn to cover them at the end of the chapter. For each fee structure, the proposed contract is given in two forms, that of the formal document and that of the informal letter of agreement. Royalties, another profitable method of remuneration, is covered in the following chapter.

But perhaps it is fitting to begin a discussion of designer's compensation with a colloquy from the famous libel trial of Whistler against Ruskin. Whistler sued Ruskin for making remarks in a review of one of his exhibitions which accused Whistler of being a mountebank who was consciously hoodwinking the public. Whistler took the stand and testified that one of the paintings in question had taken him only a little over a day to make. Ruskin's counsel asked, "And what price did you ask for it?" Whistler replied, "Two hundred guineas." Counsel asked, "Do you charge 200 guineas for two days work?" To which Whistler answered, "No, for the knowledge of a lifetime." Any method of compensating the designer must recognize that he is not only being paid for hours worked, but also "for the knowledge of a lifetime."

The Flat Fee Agreement

The flat fee contract is one in which the designer undertakes to do a specified design job for a flat price. Its chief advantage to the client is that he knows exactly how much he is going to pay for the job he has contracted, while the designer knows (or should know) the exact limits of his job and the amount of his fee.

The major pitfall of a flat fee contract to the designer is that he usually underestimates the difficulty of the job. Designers are notoriously optimistic in calculating the amount of time a job will require. In addition to this drawback, the flat fee may not take into account a project's "expandability." When a client knows that he is going to have to pay for each hour the designer spends on the job, he is naturally reluctant to needlessly multiply the hours. He will not require the designer to do modeling, detailing, etc., which can be easily handled in his own plant, and he will not require reworking of designs, submission of alternate plans, etc., unless they are clearly indicated.

But when the client is committed to only a flat fee, regardless of the time spent on the job, the client is often lavish with suggestions for revision, (which he wouldn't consider if he were charged for them) and is willing to let the designer make the models, etc. For this reason, a flat fee contract should be very specific about the number of preliminary sketches which the designer will submit, the number which will be worked into final form, who will make models, mechanicals, etc.

How much should a flat fee be? That's like asking, "How far is up?" Flat fees range from a (very) low of $100 to a student for designing or redesigning a chair, to several thousand dollars to a known-name for an entire collection. Because the flat fee is so often only a guess as to what the hourly rate would amount to, an examination of the straight-time arrangement in the following section will help the designer determine how he should estimate the flat fee.

The Proposed Contract for the Flat Fee Agreement

The proposed contract for use in a flat fee agreement that appears at the end of this chapter is based on the form originally approved by the American Society of Industrial Designers. It has since been modified in certain ways.

This is the "long form" of the formal contract and is subject to the criticisms which can be leveled against the use of such a form: it is prolix; it encourages the client to submit it to his lawyer, who may suggest changes purely for the sake of making suggestions. The chief objection is that it is more difficult to get signed because of its formidable appearance. If this form is used, it should be printed or photo-offset; this minimizes the tendency to suggest changes.

There is some difference of opinion about the effect of a WHEREAS clause that appears in the proposed form. Is it part of the agreement between the parties, or just preliminary window dressing? I once drew up a contract which said, "WHEREAS, John Doe is a well-known designer, a Fellow of the American Society of Industrial Designers, and particularly experienced in the ———— field." The designer's client made no objection to that clause, but insisted that we add another clause which said, "and WHEREAS, the CLIENT is a well-known manufacturer of ————, with a reputation for quality and integrity in said field." Of course, I agreed to the change, but to this day I don't know whether either the designer or his client got any mileage out of the two WHEREAS clauses.

There is one situation in which it does make a difference. If a stranger approaches a manufacturer and offers him an idea, and the manufacturer says, "Show it to me," the stranger can recover for the idea only if it is original and new. On the other hand, if a professional designer is hired to produce a design, it does not have to meet the same standards of novelty and originality that must be met by an outsider. The implication is that when a nonprofessional offers an idea, there is a representation that it is new and original; when you hire a professional, you are entitled only to the best professional advice. You don't expect a lawyer's brief or an accountant's advice to cover territory that is virginal. Likewise, a designer is expected to originate his design (in the sense that he doesn't copy it from someone else), but it need not necessarily be subject to copyright or patent protection, nor be new in that sense. For this reason, it is good to use the suggested WHEREAS clause.

The last paragraph of the preamble contains a blank that should be filled in with a description of the product. *Great care should be used in drawing up this description.* Both the designer and the client should know just what the job is. In many instances, the designer starts out to design one product and ends up, at the client's request, using his preliminary sketches for another product. There is no objection to this, provided it doesn't make the designer delinquent under the original agreement. It is even wise to say, "A distelfinker (or whatever the product is) to sell approximately in the $—— range." Then both parties know what the target is.

Under the first heading, "DESIGNER'S SERVICES," I like to add a first subhead: "(a) He will study the client's market and competition (and, where applicable, 'will do consumer research in connection with designs proposed by the designer')." Of course, if the research is to be anything but a cursory glance at the market, it should be calculated as a cost when the designer determines the flat fee, or as an expense to be reimbursed under 3 (B) (4) of the contract when it is contracted out to a testing or market research agency.

47

It is impossible to give a general form to cover Paragraph 1 (A) (c). Each case stands by itself. In the design of flatware (silver or stainless steel), the designer normally submits preliminary designs for three key pieces—a knife, fork, and teaspoon or tablespoon; in furniture, either a chair and a sofa or, in the case goods field, a desk; in transportation, just a single article. Of course, the client can specify as many preliminary designs as he wants, but all of this must be taken into account in fixing the fee. Similarly, the number of designs for each product is flexible: the designer can show five designs each, for each of the three key pieces, or only two. Here again, the fee should reflect the number of designs submitted.

To the requirement that the client disclose this technical data, (Para. 1 (A) (2) (a), I have added an agreement by the designer that he will treat the disclosure as confidential. If you are treated as a professional and everything is thrown open to you, your client must have confidence in the fact that he is not thereby opening his doors to the world. This is often a touchy area. If a designer becomes an expert in a field because of his services to one client, that doesn't mean that he cannot later design products for a competitor of his first client. It does, however, mean that he will not disclose to the new client any confidential matter he learned from the first client. It is sometimes difficult to draw the line between general knowledge and confidential material. What about his knowledge that certain patterns or designs sell better in the West than in the East? Or that certain colors sell better? If he gained this information because of figures disclosed by his client, is this confidential and not to be revealed to a later client in the same field, who is trying to decide between two proposed designs? Or is this general information which goes into his background of knowledge and experience permitting him to disclose it in general terms without stating confidential figures?

I have mentioned elsewhere the necessity of pinpointing the

dates on which designs are to be returned. This is very important to the designer. He has, hopefully, set aside certain time in his schedule during which he intends to complete the designs. If the client postpones making his choice, it may be weeks or months before the designer's next step is required. At that point he may be involved in other work, after having sat idle (and paid idle assistants) during a period in which he had anticipated working on the job.

If all of the designs in the original submission are rejected, the designer usually agrees to submit another batch. This is usually done without additional charge, partly because the second batch consists of designs the designer has already made but did not submit the first time around. This is not a Machiavellian ploy on the designer's part. It is inherent in the nature of the designer and the client that the designer always prefers the fresh new look, while the client is more timid and would like a design that looks almost like what sold last year or what his competitors sold last year, but is just a little bit different. I have on several occasions heard clients looking at designs say, "I've been in this business for twenty years and never sold anything like this." When asked, "Did you ever try?" they answer, "No, but I know what my customers want" (meaning the stuff they've been offered for the last twenty years). This always reminds me of the woman who said, "I know all about raising children. I've buried four of them."

Because of this difference in attitude it frequently happens that a client selects a design from the second submission which the designer rejected and withheld from the first.

It is important, in describing the working drawing (Para. 1 (A) (1) (c), to state the degree of detail that will be provided. In some cases, rough measurements will suffice; in others, micrometer exactness will be needed. It is usually easy to agree with the client on what he needs; difficulty arises only when the client first says that his engineering staff will work out those details, but, faced with a new concept, wants the designer to do the engineering. This can be avoided by a prior agreement (embodied in the indicated paragraph) on just how detailed the work is going to be and the reflection of this detail in the fee.

The client often wants exclusivity to continue beyond the period in which services are performed by the designer. For example, he may want an agreement that he won't design for a competitor for a year (or for six months) after completing the job. There is no objection to this, if the fee is fixed with this in mind and it covers not only the work needed to complete the job, but also the loss of opportunity to do work for others during the period of exclusivity.

The area of exclusivity should be defined. It should be broad enough to give the client all of the protection he needs, without unduly limiting the designer. As I stated earlier, the manufacturer of a cheap line of case goods may have no objection to the designer's working for a manufacturer of furniture in a much higher market or a manufacturer of upholstered furniture. It may even be an advantage to a manufacturer to have the designer work for a manufacturer who makes a coordinated but not competitive line, so that each line will help promote the other.

I do not like the cancellation clause (Para. 4). It tempts the client to break the job down into phases and to pay the designer for the first phase (or the first two phases) and complete the job himself, once he knows just what sort of design the designer has in mind. This has several unhappy results. It deprives the designer of part of his compensation, although he has already parted with the most creative part of his work; it often results in a job the designer is not proud of, because the preliminary designs are not executed under his supervision and are often perverted in execution. I have therefore added to this clause the final sentence which makes it clear that, if cancellation takes place before the job is done, the designs remain the property of the designer. This gives the client a way out if he is not happy with the designs, but does not permit him to cancel and nevertheless use the designs.

The patent and copyright clause also bothers me a little. I have no objection to an exclusive license to the client in this field, but a complete assignment may be unwise. Suppose a designer created the first aerosol for a shaving cream manufacturer. Should he assign the patent completely, so that it covered the use of the aerosol mechanism for paints, furniture polish, deodorants, whipped cream, and the thousands of other uses? I have added to Paragraph 5 (A) (2) the words "in the client's business," but perhaps there should be an even narrower limitation.

The use of the designer's name may be of great importance to the designer. I endorse the requirement that its use may be limited to products which meet the quality of the standard sample. But as originally drawn, the contract merely provided that if this quality were not met, the designer's name would be removed. This had two bad effects—the designer lost the requirement that his name be used, and he also lost the psychic return of seeing a good design well executed. I have added to this clause a requirement that the client use his best efforts to bring the quality back to the standard as soon as he can.

The remaining clauses are "boiler plate" but desirable. I suggest one additional clause: "Although this agreement calls for design services, it is not a personal service contract and the death, disability, or inability to perform by the Designer or any member of his firm shall not terminate the obligations of the client hereunder, it being understood that performance hereunder may be by the Designer or by his employees designated by him." This protects the designer from an attempt to cancel if he is ill, disabled, or dead. His office should be able to carry on and fulfill the contract in his stead.

Form: Standard Contract for Flat Fee Agreement

AGREEMENT BETWEEN _____

_____

AND _____

THIS AGREEMENT, made as of the _____

day of _____ 19 _____, by and between _____

_____

_____ of _____

_____ (hereinafter called the "Designer")

and _____

of _____ (hereinafter called the "Client"),

WITNESSETH:

WHEREAS, _____

is a professional designer and a member in good standing of the
Industrial Designers Society of America, and

WHEREAS, the Client desires to obtain the Designer's services as
outlined below;

NOW, THEREFORE, in consideration of the mutual understandings herein contained, the parties agree as follows:

The Client hereby engages the Designer's services from the date
hereof until the date of completion of the services set forth below,
for the purpose of designing _____
hereinafter referred to as the "product."

1. DESIGNER'S SERVICES:

(A) Submission of Preliminary Designs:

(1) In this connection, the Designer agrees that:

(a) He will confer with the Client or his representatives
with respect to the price range, type of product,
and general requirements of the product.

(b) He will make any trips to the Client's factory mutually considered reasonable and necessary, to study
limitations of production methods.

(c) He will, on or before _____ submit to the
Client, in _____ form, _____
designs for the product.

(2) In this connection, the Client agrees that:

(a) It will supply the Designer with all the technical

data and facilities necessary for the effective performance of the Designer's services, and will acquaint him with all previous or current developments in the field of the product. The Designer agrees to treat all such disclosures as confidential.

  (b) It will, within _____ days of their submission by the Designer, indicate, in writing, approval or rejection of the designers.

(3) If the Client rejects all of the designs, the Designer agrees to submit _____ additional designs within _____ after receipt of notice of the rejection.

(B) Submission of Working Drawings and Models: Upon written approval of the designs by the Client, the Designer agrees to submit working drawings and/or models of the approved design(s) within _____ .

(C) Criticism of Factory Samples:

The Designer agrees to work with the Client in developing final designs for the product, and to supervise and criticize models or samples in order that corrections may be made before full-scale manufacture is undertaken.

2. EXCLUSIVITY:

The designer will undertake no work for anyone else in the field of _____ while he is performing the services set forth in Paragraph 1 above.

3. REMUNERATION:

  (A) For the services outlined above, the Client agrees to pay the Designer a flat fee in the amount of _____ dollars ($), payable _____

  (B) The following will be billed by the Designer to the Client and paid for as extras; these charges will be billed at cost, without any added percentage for overhead or handling:

    (1) Traveling costs and expenses incidental thereto, but only when incurred at the request or on the authorization of the Client.

(2) Telephone toll charges.

(3) Extra blueprints.

(4) (Model making, samples, new materials, etc.)

(5) _____

_____

4. CANCELLATION:

    (A) This contract shall terminate when the Designer has completed the services set forth in Paragraph 1 above.

    (B) The Client may, by notice in writing, terminate this contract after the submission by the Designer of preliminary designs, in which event the flat fee due the designer shall be _____ ($); or after the submission of working drawings and models, in which case the fee shall be _____ dollars ($); in either event simultaneously with the written notice, which shall be given _____ after the submission of the designs or drawings and models by the Designer. In the event of such termination all rights in the designs shall remain with the Designer.

5. GENERAL CONDITIONS:

    (A) Rights in the Design:

        (1) The designs submitted by the Designer for said line shall be and remain the property of the Designer, together with any and all drawings, models, and samples furnished by the Designer, subject to the exclusive right to manufacture, sell, and distribute the accepted designs herein granted to the Client, so long as the Client is not in default of its obligations under this contract, nor shall have terminated this contract under Paragraph 4.

        (2) The Client shall have the right to have the designs or any one of them copyrighted or patented in the United States in the Designer's name, but at the Client's expense; and the Designer agrees to give the Client every cooperation necessary and desirable in order to enable it to procure such copyright or patent. The Designer

agrees to license the Client during the term of this agreement, or so long as the Client is not in default of payments hereunder, to use the designs covered by such patent or copyright in the Client's business.

(3) If such designs or processes or any of them shall be copyrighted or patented, the Client may at his option sue to enforce or protect said copyright or patent and in such event the Designer agrees to join in or bring such action for damages or injunction as the Client may direct, the Client at all times to hold the Designer free and harmless from costs and expenses in connection with same. In all such events, the Designer will employ such counsel as the Client may direct, and all recoveries shall be received by the Designer for the Client's benefit and turned over to the Client, except that the portion of the net recovery, if any, representing payment due the Designer shall be retained by, or paid to, the Designer.

The Client may use the Designer's name in connection with the product, subject to the following restrictions:

(1) Such name may be so used only after the Designer has given written approval of the manner in which the designs and finishes have been executed.

(2) As each factory sample is received, the Designer will promptly criticize or approve it in writing. If, in the opinion of the Designer, the appearance of any product as manufactured in regular production is not equivalent to that contained in the standard samples as approved by the Designer, the Designer may, in writing, call for the removal of his name from the article, and the Client shall not use the Designer's name in connection therewith until the appearance again meets with the Designer's approval. The Client agrees to use his best efforts to keep and bring the regular production up to the quality of the standard sample.

(3) The Client agrees to submit the copy and art work for

all such advertisement and promotional literature to the Designer for his approval before final printing or issuance thereof.

(C) Modification:

This agreement is the entire understanding between the parties, and no modification or change herein shall be effective unless in writing and executed by both parties hereto.

(D) Insolvency:

Should the Client be liquidated or become bankrupt or insolvent, or be reorganized under the Bankruptcy Act, the right to use the Designer's designs shall not be sold or transferred except subject to the provisions of this agreement.

(E) Arbitration:

Any dispute arising under or in connection with this agreement shall be arbitrated before the American Arbitration Association in the City of _____ pursuant to the rules and regulations of that body then in effect.

(F) Assignment:

This agreement shall not be assigned by either party without the other's consent. In the event that a party is succeeded by another by operation of law, this contract shall be binding upon and inure to the benefit of such successors.

(G) Additional Services:

Any services by the Designer not specifically set forth herein shall be compensated for separately, as agreed upon by the parties hereto before being undertaken or, if no such prior arrangement is made at the Designer's usual rates.

(H) Additional Terms:

_____

_____

_____

_____

_____

at _____ State of _____

IN WITNESS WHEREOF, the parties hereto have executed this agreement on the _____ day of _____ nineteen hundred and _____ .

By: _____

                                     Designer

                                     Title

By: _____

                                     Title

                                     Client

Form: Letter for Flat Fee Agreement

Gentlemen:

I am pleased that you have decided to have me design your new _____, and I am writing this letter to set forth the terms of our collaboration. I have several exciting ideas about this project and am eager to get started on it.

I will study your market and competition and your production facilities in order to design a _____ to sell in the $_____ range. You will make available to me your present, past and planned models. I will treat all information received from you as confidential. On or before the _____ day of _____, I will submit _____ preliminary sketches (of three key pieces, or what have you).

You agree to select the approved design and make any suggestions for changes within _____ days of my submission. Within _____ weeks thereafter I will submit finished drawings in _____ form adequate for your production facilities. I will follow the designs through production and make any changes necessary to eliminate "bugs" that crop up in the course of production. I will approve a standard sample of the prototype.

So long as the goods produced by you conform in quality to the standard sample, I will permit you (and you agree) to use my name in a form approved by me, on every piece of merchandise using my designs (by hang tag or label).

I will advise you on merchandising, packaging and advertising the line I design, but if you want me to design any packaging, typography or advertising, those services will be the subject of a separate agreement.

If my designs are capable of copyright, patent or similar protection, I will, at your request and expense, secure such protection and execute without further fee, an exclusive license to you to use these rights in your field.

You have agreed to pay me for my services as designer, $_____, payable in monthly installments, commencing _____ of $_____. I will bill you and you will pay me for travel expenses (including living expenses while traveling), long distance telephone calls,

58

messenger service, telegrams, extra blueprints and drawings, mod-elling costs, _____, and other out-of-pocket expenses, but will incur no such expenses in excess of $50. each without your approval.

In order that we may both have a copy of this agreement, I have prepared it in duplicate. If you agree to its terms, please sign and return the enclosed carbon, so that I can start at once on this project.

I look forward to a pleasant and mutually profitable relation-ship with you.

Faithfully yours,

AGREED TO:
Blank Co.
By _____, Dated:

If an arbitration clause is to be included, insert:
We have agreed that any dispute arising out of this agreement shall be submitted to arbitration, under the rules then in effect, of the American Arbitration Association.

If exclusivity is bargained and paid for, insert:
During the year on which I work on your project, and for _____ months thereafter, I will not design any _____ for any of your competitors (in the $_____ market).

Or: If, within _____ months of completion of my contract, I contemplate designing any _____ for the $_____ market, I will give you the right of first refusal to enter an agree-ment whereby I will design them for you.

The Straight-Time Arrangement

In the foregoing, I discussed and included forms for a flat fee contract (one in which the fee is an agreed-upon flat price). In this chapter, we are concerned with a contract in which the compensation is at an hourly rate, the straight-time contract.

The chief advantage of the straight-time arrangement is that the risk to the designer is minimized. Even if he has been overly optimistic about the speed with which the design job can be accomplished, he will receive the proper full hourly rate for every hour spent on the job. On the other hand, many clients are hesitant to enter straight-time agreements unless the designer places a ceiling on the job. If such a ceiling is placed, the contract becomes a "heads I win, tails you lose" proposition. If the job is done in a very short time, the designer's pay is little unless a minimum price is provided, as it is in the suggested form following this chapter. If the job takes so much time that the ceiling comes into operation, the designer works for the excess hours without pay (or the job is never finished).

One compromise that has usually been acceptable is for the designer to agree to keep the client informed of the number of hours already spent on the job by regular (often weekly) reports. If the client finds that the budgetary limit is being neared, he may request the designer to hurry the job, or to skip certain details, in the interest of keeping costs within the estimates. But he will not abandon the project. Once he has put so much cost into the design job, he will not throw this money away, by directing the designer not to complete the job. He is more likely to scrounge enough money to finish the job in order to save the investment he has already committed.

Another objection to the time rate of compensation is that it rewards mediocrity. A designer who fumbles for weeks only to come up with a mediocre design gets paid more than one who produces an excellent design in a flash of brilliance. While the example may be extreme, there is the danger that inspiration may be penalized by the time rate and dullness rewarded by it. One large design studio has a unique solution to this problem. It charges two rates. One is a fee for "design," which is a flat fee for the creative solution to the project. In addition, it charges a straight hourly rate, which is moderate and is designed to cover working-time costs. If this office reaches a quick solution, it makes its profit on the design fee and the client saves money on the time rate. On the other hand, if an unusually long time is taken by the project, the designer's profit (the design fee) remains the same, but the client's charges are kept down by the low hourly rate.

Determining Hourly Rates

What is a fair hourly rate? The conventional practice is to charge three times the payroll cost of the man whose time is being figured. Thus, a renderer whose salary is $120 for a forty-hour week (amounting to $3.00 per hour) will be charged out at $9.00 per hour. The theory is that the office charges out the time at cost, to cover its direct cost, doubles it to cover overhead, and triples it to cover idle time, profit, etc.

At first glance, tripling the cost of time seems high to the purchaser. But on examination it will appear to be a bargain.

The client may be buying only several hundred hours of work a year. If he hired an employee, he'd have to give 2,000 hours of work a year, pay for vacation, sickness, and holidays, as well as for social security and workman's compensation. He would have to supply office and work space, stenographic and reception services at present high rates, perhaps cover the worker under pension and profit-sharing plans, and would, finally, have to pay him not only for actual working time, but also for the time spent between jobs contemplating his navel.

Even without considering the desirability of having an outside designer (who is free from the inhibitions inherent in being a staff member and who brings experience from other jobs, plus the general yeastiness rising from being a designer in multiple fields)—even without these considerations, it is a bargain to buy design services at three times their cost from the design studio. The going rate per hour depends on whether you are paying the nadir in rendering services or the acme of design creativity: current rates run from about $10 an hour to as much as $60 an hour for some studio chiefs who may spend only a few hours per job reviewing and editing staff presentations. Some design offices average their hourly rate and charge the average rate regardless of the workers involved.

Architectural Offices

Architectural offices usually charge 2-1/2 times the base pay of their employees. This is because once the monumental aspect of a design is established, the employees who do the "envelope stuffing" are kept busy full time for an extended period on their drafting and similar work. This has two results: there is little time lost because an employee does several jobs during a week. An architectural job keeps the worker occupied on the one job for an extensive period. Also, the work of the studio chief is less varied. Once a job is assigned to an employee, he can be kept on the job with less moment-to-moment supervision than if he were designing a series of products in an industrial design office. The lesson to be learned from this distinction in rates is that a design job which occupies workers full time for an extended period may command a lower hourly rate than one which is neither a full-time nor a long-time job.

The third multiple of the salary paid covers not only idle time, and profit, but the studio head's time as entrepreneur (which is properly part of his overhead cost). Time spent in interviewing and hiring help, bird-dogging new work, managing the office, etc., is covered by this third mark-up. Actual time spent at the drafting board, conferring with the client, or editing work of employees on the job is charged out to the client as time spent by the studio head.

What rate should the studio head charge per hour? He should figure his draw just as though it were a paid salary. If he draws, say, $400 a week, that's $10 an hour and his time should be charged out at $30 per hour.

Contract for Straight-Time Agreement

In performing under a straight-time contract, it is obvious that accurate time records must be kept by each person working on the job. I have never had a client question a designer's time records, but this is probably because all of the designers with whom I have worked submitted detailed time breakdowns as part of their billing.

The form contract set forth at the end of this chapter is almost identical with the form recommended by the American Society of Industrial Designers (now IDSA) and the following comments are pertinent:

The WHEREAS clauses might very well contain a statement that the client is a manufacturer (or distributor) of the goods covered by the agreement. If he has certain facilities for manufacture, the designer or client may want a statement to that effect because the design should be conceived within the limits of the client's ability to manufacture the product with existing facilities, or with facilities reasonably available by purchase or by subcontracting.

Paragraph 1: The job should be described in sufficient detail so that there is no room for disagreement about the scope of the designer's responsibility. Subsection (c) should detail the form in which early presentations are to be made and (d) the form in which final presentation is to be made; (e) should, where applicable, indicate whether models are to be made by the designer or by the staff of the client, and that the client is to pay for any modeling costs incurred outside of the client's plant.

Paragraph 2, (b): If the client is to have exclusivity of the designer's services in a certain field, the field should be specifically described. It should be large enough to protect the client, but no larger. This field can often be defined by price levels. A client usually has little objection to a designer's working for another manufacturer who makes products that are so much more high-priced than his line that they are not really competitive. In fact, as mentioned earlier, he may welcome such activity as adding prestige to the line designed for him. Remember that by giving exclusivity you are cutting yourself off from a part of your market. It should, therefore, not be given unless the minimum fee (see Paragraph 3) is high enough to warrant the sacrifice of potential business.

The use of name: The form merely gives the client the right to use the designer's name. Some designers require its use. This identifies their designs and avoids confusion with other (often less fortunate) designs sold by the same manufacturer.

Paragraph 4: There may be other incidental expenses. I sometimes provide that all out-of-pocket expenses incurred for the client will be reimbursed, and I add, to protect the client, that no such expenses in excess of, say, $25 per item will be incurred without the authorization of the client. This nominal *carte blanche* makes it unnecessary to go hat in hand to the client to secure approval, for example, of a $5 messenger cost when time is pressing and the designer knows that this cost is justified.

I do not feel that the option of renewal gives either side anything valuable. If the client wants to renew at a lower rate, he will not hesitate to suggest it; if rates have gone up, the renewal clause may prove to be a handicap to the designer.

Rights in the Designs

Most clients who have paid the full consideration stipulated in an agreement will insist that the designs are theirs. The designer may, nevertheless, require that their integrity be preserved. If the designs are identified by the trade or the public with the designer, he is entitled to protection against changes in the design which might reflect adversely on his reputation. However, the client's right to use the designs should not be limited (as in the form) to "the term of the agreement."

Likewise, there will be difficulty in getting a client to agree to subsection (d) of Paragraph 6. While a designer works for psychic as well as material returns, and wants to see his designs in production, very few clients will agree to a clause which provides that after a designer has been paid in full, he may recapture his designs because the client has dragged his feet about putting it into production. On the other hand, most clients will agree to a clause which gives the designer back his designs if the project is abandoned before the designer is paid in full. Of course, where the designer's compensation depends on the sale of the goods embodying the designs (as, for instance, in a royalty contract), a clause re-vesting the designs in the designer on the manufacturer's failure to make the merchandise is fair.

Some contracts provide for a cut-off after the operation of

Paragraph 1 (d), or 1 (c). Thus, if after the first presentation or the second, the client decides that he doesn't want to go ahead with the project, he can buy his release from the contract by making an additional payment (agreed upon in advance) to the designer. The purpose of this payment is to compensate the designer for the loss involved in abandoning the project and changing over his help and studio activity to another job.

I would suggest adding to Paragraph 1 a clause which requires the designer "to keep the client informed of the progress of the work hereunder, and to furnish, from time to time, estimates (which shall be made in good faith but shall not be binding on the designer) of the amount of time necessary to complete the work." This will enable the client to exercise some budgetary control over the job. If this clause were added, the maximum in Paragraph 3 might very well be stricken.

Form: **Standard Contract for Straight-Time Agreement**

AGREEMENT BETWEEN _____

AND _____

THIS AGREEMENT, made as of the _____

day of _____ 19 _____, by and between _____

_____ of _____

_____ (hereinafter called the "Designer")

and _____

of _____ (hereinafter called the "Client"),

WITNESSETH:

WHEREAS, _____

is a professional designer and a member in good standing of the
Industrial Designer's Society of America, engaged in the field of
industrial design; and

WHEREAS, the Client desires to obtain the Designer's services in
designing certain products, and the exclusive right to his services
in the field of _____

NOW, THEREFORE, in consideration of the mutual undertakings
herein contained, the parties agree that:

1. SERVICES:

The Client hereby engages the Designer's services to design

_____

_____

_____

_____

to be manufactured, distributed, and sold by the Client or for
its account. Said designs are hereinafter referred to as the "designs" and the products embodying the designs as the "product"
or "products." The Designer shall commence work on the designing of said product on or before _____

_____, and shall submit each design with a space provided
on the reverse side thereof for the Client's acceptance or rejection, and the Client shall signify its acceptance or rejection of
each design within _____

of receipt of same by signing in the space provided therefor, and immediately returning rejected designs to the Designer. All designs not returned within the period limited shall be deemed accepted by the Client. If all designs are rejected, the Designer shall, within _____, submit additional designs. The Client shall have no rights in connection with any rejected designs.

In connection with the design of said products, the Designer further agrees:

(a) to confer with any representatives designated by the Client with respect to the type of merchandise required for manufacture and the price range desired;

(b) to make trips to the Client's factory, when mutually considered necessary and reasonable, to study limitations of production methods;

(c) at the request of the Client, to submit various designs as described above for said products, such designs to be presented on or before _____, in the form of _____;

(d) after the selection of designs for production by the Client, and notification thereof to the Designer, sufficiently to complete the designs selected and deliver to the Client within _____ weeks, said designs in the form of _____;

(e) to work with the Client in developing final designs for said products, and promptly supervise and criticize models or samples in order that corrections may be made before full-scale manufacture is undertaken;

(f) when requested by the Client, to consult on matters pertaining to the packaging and display of said designs;

(g) to consult with the Client or its agency and criticize (but not design) the art work, layouts, and copy for promotional material, such as flyers, advertisements, and advertisement mats, in connection with the products manufactured from said designs.

In order to expedite the designing of said products, the Client will cooperate with the Designer and will supply the Designer and his assistants at all times with all technical data necessary to the effective performance of the Designer's services, and to acquaint the Designer with all previous or current developments or designing work on the problems submitted to him. The Designer agrees that all information received from the Client will be treated as confidential and not divulged.

2. EXCLUSIVE LICENSE:

The Designer hereby gives and grants to the Client, and the Client hereby accepts from the Designer, all upon the terms and conditions herein set forth, the sole and exclusive right, license, and privilege:

    (a) to manufacture, sell and distribute, in domestic and foreign markets, products embodying the designs to be furnished to it by the Designer hereunder:

    (b) to reserve the exclusive use of the Designer's services in the field of _____ for the period from _____ to _____; and the Designer agrees that during that period he will not design such products for manufacture by any other than the Client. However, nothing contained in this paragraph shall prevent the Designer from designing for other manufacturers, _____

_____

    (c) to use the Designer's name in the marketing, sale, and distribution of said products, subject to the following restrictions:

      (1) Such name may be so used only after the Designer has given written approval of the manner in which the designs and finishes have been executed.

      (2) As each factory sample is received the Designer will promptly criticize or approve it in writing.

      (3) If, in the opinion of the Designer, the appearance of any products as manufactured in regular production is not equivalent to that contained in the standard samples as approved by the Designer, the Designer may, in writing,

call for the removal of his name from the article and the Client will not use the Designer's name in connection therewith until the appearance again meets with the Designer's approval. The Client agrees, in such event, to use its best efforts to remedy any defects in the product.

(4) The Client agrees to submit the copy and art work for all such advertisements and promotional literature to the Designer for his approval before the final printing or issuance thereof.

3. REMUNERATION:

The Client will pay the Designer for the time spent by the Designer and his staff in creating said design, at the following rates:

_____

_____

_____

_____

_____

The total charges under this paragraph shall in no event be less than:

_____ dollars ($) or exceed
_____ dollars ($) without the
prior written authorization of the Client.

The Designer has already submitted to the Client an estimate of the amount of time required to perfect the designs. The Client will be billed _____, and will pay said bills within five days of receipt of same.

4. TRAVEL AND INCIDENTAL EXPENSES:

Extra blueprints, all long distance telephone charges, traveling costs, and expenses incidental thereto, shall be billed to the Client as extras; but shall be billed at actual cost, with no added percentage for overhead or profit. Travel costs and expenses will be incurred only when and to the extent that they have been authorized by the Client. The Designer will keep long distance charges to a reasonable amount.

5. OPTIONAL OF RENEWAL:

The Client may renew this contract, including the right to the exclusive services of the Designer in the designated field, by notifying the Designer on or before _____ and guaranteeing to him payment of _____ ($_____) for the services during the period of said renewal and paying said amount on or before _____. If either the notice of renewal or guarantee or payment are not received by the Designer on the date specified, the Designer will be free from the restrictions on his services set forth in this contract.

6. RIGHTS IN THE DESIGNS:

(a) The designs submitted by the Designer for said products shall be and remain the property of the Designer, together with any and all drawings, models, and samples furnished by the Designer, subject to the exclusive right to manufacture, sell, and distribute the accepted designs herein granted to the Client, so long as the Client is not in default of its obligations under this contract. _____ shall have the right to possession of all designs and models.

(b) The Client shall have the right to have the designs or any one of them copyrighted or patented with the Goverment of the United States in the Designer's name, but at the Client's expense; and the Designer shall give the Client every cooperation necessary and desirable in order to enable it to procure such copyright or patent. The Designer agrees to license the Client during the term of this agreement, or so long as the Client is not in default of payment, to use the designs covered by such patent or copyright.

(c) If such designs or processes or any of them shall be copyrighted or patented, the Client may at its option sue to enforce or protect said copyright or patent, and in such event the Designer agrees to join in or bring such action for damages or injunction as the Client may direct, the Client at all times to hold the Designer free and harmless from costs and expenses in connection with same. In all such events, the Designer will employ such counsel as the Client may direct, and all recoveries shall be received by the Designer for the Client's benefit and turned over to the Client.

(d) Should accepted designs not be produced and marketed by the Client within _____ of the date hereof, possession of the designs shall be returned to the Designer, the license to manufacture same shall terminate, and the Designer shall have the right to make any use whatsoever of such designs. The termination of the license under this clause shall not terminate the obligation of the Client to pay any amounts due or to become due under this contract.

(e) In the event that the manufacture of said products is prevented, hindered, or delayed by strikes, fires, floods, or by any similar circumstances beyond the control of the Client, the periods of limitation provided herein for the commencement of manufacture of said products shall be extended by the time during which the manufacture of said products is so prevented, hindered or delayed.

7. MODIFICATION OR CHANGE OF AGREEMENT:

This agreement is the entire understanding between the parties, and no modification or change in this agreement shall be effective unless in writing and executed by both parties hereto.

8. INSOLVENCY:

Should the Client be liquidated, or become bankrupt or insolvent, or be reorganized under Chapter X or any other provision of the Bankruptcy Act, right to the use of the Designer's designs cannot be sold unless they are subject to all provisions of this agreement.

9. ASSIGNMENT OF CONTRACT:

This agreement shall not be assigned by either party without the written consent of the other, but in the event of either party being succeeded by another by the operation of law, this contract shall be binding upon and inure to the benefit of such successor. The Designer may assign payments due to him under this contract by written notice to the Client.

10. ARBITRATION:

Any and all disputes and controversies arising hereunder or in connection herewith shall be submitted to the American Arbitration Association for arbitration, pursuant to the rules and regulations of that body then obtaining. The cost of arbitration shall be borne equally by both parties and the decision of the arbitrator shall be binding and conclusive upon them.

11. ADDITIONAL TERMS:

_____

_____

_____

_____

_____

_____

_____

_____

_____

IN WITNESS WHEREOF, the parties here to have executed this agreement on the _____ day of _____, nineteen hundred and _____.

_____

Designer

_____

Client

Form: Letter for Straight-Time Agreement

Gentlemen:

I am pleased that you have decided to have me design your new _____, and I am writing this letter to set forth the terms of our collaboration. I have exciting ideas about this project and am eager to get started on it.

I will study your market, competition, and your production facilities in order to design a _____ to sell in the $_____ range. You will make available to me your present, past and planned models. I will treat all information received from you as confidential. On or before the _____ day of _____, I will submit _____ preliminary sketches (of three key pieces, or what have you).

You agree to select the approved design and make any suggestions for changes within _____ days of my submission. Within _____ weeks thereafter I will submit finished drawings in _____ form adequate for your production facilities. I will follow the designs through production and make any changes necessary to eliminate "bugs" that crop up in the course of production. I will approve a standard sample of the prototype.

So long as the goods produced by you conform in quality to the standard sample, I will permit you (and you agree) to use my name in a form approved by me, on every piece of merchandise using my design (by hang tag or label). If the quality falls below that of the standard sample, I will inform you and you agree to remove my name until the quality is reinstated. You agree to use your best efforts to restore the quality as soon as possible.

I will advise you on merchandising, packaging and advertising the line I design, but if you want me to design any packaging, typography or advertising, those services will be the subject of a separate agreement.

If my designs are capable of copyright, patent or similar protection, I will, at your request and expense, secure such protection and execute without further fee, an exclusive license to you to use these rights in your field.

You have agreed to pay, for the time spent on executing these designs, (including time spent consulting with you and your staff) at the rate of $_____ an hour for chief designers, and $_____ an hour for staff (perhaps $_____ an hour for mechanicals or paste-ups should be added where applicable).

You will also reimburse me for all out-of-pocket expenses, such as travel and expenses while traveling, telegrams, messenger service, extra blue prints, model-making, etc., but no such expenses in excess of $_____ each will be charged to you without your approval.

I will keep you informed, each week, of the approximate hours and expense incurred to date, so that you may schedule the work with your budget in mind, and be kept aware of the progress of the work.

I am very enthusiastic about the possibilities of this program and of working with your staff on this interesting project. In order that we may both have a copy of this letter, I have prepared a duplicate. If the terms are satisfactory to you, please sign and return the enclosed carbon copy.

Very truly yours,

AGREED TO:
XYZ Company
By _____

Date:

An arbitration clause and exclusivity clause can be added to this form if wanted.

The Retainer Agreement

A retainer agreement is simply a flat fee or straight-time agreement, spread out over a period of time. This assures the designer of a guaranteed income during the retainer period, and usually reserves the services of the designer (including any ideas which he develops in the client's field) for the period of the retainer.

If a retainer agreement is a modified flat fee agreement, it will provide for the fee to be paid in installments over the retainer period. If it is a modified straight-time agreement, it will provide for the use of the designer's services for a minimum of so many hours (or days) each month (or week) during the period of the retainer. In fairness to the designer, it should provide for payment for any time in excess of the guaranteed minimum which the designer is called upon to spend on the client's work.

One difficulty that sometimes arises in retainer agreements is that the retainer is not used for some months, and more hours than the retainer hours are required in other months. I suggest a carry-over, something like a loss carry-over used for tax purposes. For example, a retainer may call for the designer to devote, say, 50 hours a month to the client's work. During a slack season his services may be used for only 30 hours, but he will be paid for 50 hours. The contract may provide that no more than 20 hours unused in any month may be carried forward for one month only. This gives the client an opportunity to smooth out some of the troughs and crests in his use of the designer. But the carry-over should not be too large or for too long a period, lest the designer find himself at the end of a year subject to supplying 400 hours worth of work in the final month.

Some retainers are for a definite period and terminate automatically. I prefer to make them for a minimum period, but to provide for automatic renewal from period to period unless either party gives the other, say, 30 days' notice of intention to terminate. These make it unnecessary for the designer to go hat in hand for a renewal at regular intervals; it keeps him interested in the job and with his mind on his work instead of worrying about renewals. But it permits either the client or the designer to terminate or renegotiate after the expiration of the minimum period of time.

In the retainer contract form following this chapter, Section 2 provides for a fee for "general availability" of the designer and for additional pay for all work done by staff. I suggest that it is fairer to both designer and client to have the retainer cover a certain number of minimum hours of the time of the designer and his staff, with the carry-over provision which I mentioned above.

I also suggest that the first sentence of Paragraph 1 be changed to read, "The designer will, during the period of this contract," instead of limiting the retainer to a year. Paragraph 6 (TERMINATION) should then be changed to read: "This agreement may be terminated by either party after six months from the date of its inception, by ninety (90) days' notice in writing," etc.

Form: Standard Contract for Retainer Agreement

AGREEMENT BETWEEN _____

AND _____

THIS AGREEMENT, made as of the _____

day of _____ 19 _____, by and between _____

_____ of _____

_____ (hereinafter called the "Designer")

and _____

of _____ (hereinafter called the "Client"),

WITNESSETH:

WHEREAS, _____

is a professional designer and a member in good standing of the
Industrial Designers Society of America, engaged in the field of
industrial design; and

WHEREAS, the Client desires to obtain the Designer's services in
designing certain products, and the exclusive right to his services
in the field of _____

NOW, THEREFORE, in consideration of the promises, covenants,
and undertakings herein contained, the parties agree as follows:

1. DESIGNER'S SERVICES:

The Designer will, for a period of one year from the date of this
agreement,

   (a) Study and familiarize himself with the design problems re-
       lating to the _____ of the Client, includ-
       ing the existing line, competitive products, production lim-
       itations and possibilities, new developments, and general
       merchandising problems;

   (b) Confer with the representatives of the Client with respect
       to the type of merchandise and packaging required by the
       Client, and the price range desired;

   (c) Make trips to the Client's factory, when mutually con-
       sidered necessary and reasonable, to study limitation of
       production methods;

(d) At the request of the Client, submit various designs for said _____ ;

(e) After selection of designs by the Client and notification thereof to the Designer, sufficiently complete the designs selected and deliver to the Client said designs in the form of _____ ;

(f) Work with the Client in developing final designs for said products, and promptly supervise and criticize models or samples in order that corrections may be made before full-scale manufacture is undertaken.

(g) When requested by the Client, consult on matters pertaining to the packaging and display of products using said designs, and execute same.

2. REMUNERATION:

(a) The Client will pay to the Designer an annual fee of _____ _____ dollars ($), in monthly installments of _____ dollars ($), payable on the _____ of each month, commencing _____ . This will cover the general availability and attention of the Designer, all services rendered by him, and the exclusive right to his services in the field.

(b) The Client will also pay to the Designer monthly, within _____ of billing, his expenses, including the charges for work done by members of the Designer's staff, at cost plus a percentage for overhead, for consultation, supervision of manufacturing processes, drafting, modeling, and lettering (list to be completed as fits the situation). Models and other direct expenses outside the Designer's studio, including consultants retained with the consent of the Client, will be paid for at cost plus _____ per cent (%). Travel expenses, telephone tolls, and _____ will be paid for at cost, but no traveling expenses will be incurred without the prior approval of the Client.

3. EXCLUSIVITY:

During the period of this agreement, and for _____
_____ thereafter, the Designer will not design any _____
_____ for any other Client (but this agreement
shall not limit his right to design _____).
The Client will not during this period, retain any industrial designer other than the Designer in connection with its _____
_____ without notifying the Designer (but this
shall not prevent it from employing designers on its staff).

4. RIGHTS IN THE DESIGNS:

All designs executed and used in products of the Client during
the period of this contract shall become and remain the property
of the Client, but any designs, ideas, sketches, or suggestions
of the Designer or his staff not used by the Client during the
period of this agreement shall remain the property of the Designer. The Designer will treat as confidential any information
about manufacturing processes, trade secrets, plans of the Client,
etc., disclosed by the Client. The Designer will cooperate with
the Client in any patent, copyright, or trade mark application
made by the Client and in any suits for infringement, unfair competition, etc., brought by the Client, but all such cooperation
shall be at the Client's expense. Nothing in this paragraph shall
give the Client any rights in the name of the Designer.

5. DESIGNER'S NAME:

The Client may use the name of the Designer in connection with
its products only on the prior written consent of the Designer and
his approval of the product, advertisement, release, or publicity
containing such name.

6. TERMINATION:

This agreement may be terminated by the Client upon ninety
(90) days' notice in writing, but such termination shall not release
the Client from his obligation to pay the monthly installments
which shall become due on account of the retainer of the Designer during such ninety (90) day period.

7. MODIFICATION OF AGREEMENT:

This is the entire understanding of the parties, and no modification or change herein shall be effective unless in writing and executed by both parties hereto.

8. ARBITRATION:

Any dispute or controversy arising under or in connection with this contract shall be submitted for arbitration in the City of _____, before the American Arbitration Association, pursuant to the rules and regulations of that body then obtaining.

9. ASSIGNMENT:

Neither party hereto shall assign this agreement without the consent of the other; but if either party is succeeded by another by operation of law, this agreement shall be binding upon and inure to the benefit of the successor.

10. ADDITIONAL TERMS:

_____

IN WITNESS WHEREOF, the parties hereto have executed this agreement on the _____ day of _____, nineteen hundred and _____.

_____
Designer

_____
Client

Consultation and
Other Agreements

A designer may be called upon for a single consultation. This may call for a brief study of a line (or of the competition's) and a written report, recommending a course of action. It is sometimes argued that most consultations amount to a fee for the designer to recommend a new design program, to be executed by himself. But, in many instances, designers who have been hired as consultants have recommended abandonment of the project they were consulted about, or preservation of the status quo, or the retention of another designer.

As in all design contracts, the consultation agreement should describe carefully the area of consultation, and just what the designer is going to do. Will he report only his general recommendation or will he outline a detailed design program? A great deal of misunderstanding can be avoided if the details of the consultation are agreed upon in advance and set forth in the contract.

What fee should be charged for a consultation? The hourly charge for a limited one-shop job should be much higher than

82

for a long-term undertaking. A fee of $1000 a day is not un-
heard of for consultation, but $250 a day (covering both study
of the problem and preparation of the report) is probably
more usual. The fee to be charged (like that of a surgeon) will
depend on the importance of the consultation to the client:
the client's ability to pay and the probable productivity of the
report are among the factors that will help determine the fee.

Access to Previous Design Work

I recommended that a paragraph be added to the consultation contract form, which would state: "You agree to open
your files to me and give me complete information about the
such-and-such problem, including the work done to date and
the designs offered by your competition, and I agree to treat
as confidential all disclosures made by you to me."

This clause will avoid the fiasco that would result if the
designer, after studying the problem, came up with a solution
which the client already had in its files, or had tried (or considered) and previously rejected.

The note to the approved form says: "A consultation is
usually preliminary, and anticipates a longer relationship if
the consultation is successful." It is probably easier, during
these preliminaries, to enter into a letter agreement, drawing
up a more formal agreement later, if needed. The form printed
with this text is the approved letter agreement, but should
be fleshed out with a detailed description of the project.

Building agreements, covering alterations, construction, etc.,
may be covered by the printed form contracts of the American
Institute of Architects, from whom they are available at a
modest charge. While these contracts describe the designer as
"architect," I have used them in the form in which they are
printed by adding a clause which states: "Although John Doe
is designated as 'architect' in this agreement, both parties recognize that he is not an architect nor licensed to act as such,

but that this designation is used merely for convenience. In the event that the rules of any governmental or administrative body or any applicable statute or law require the signature or approval of a registered architect on plans, specifications, drawings or the like, John Doe will secure such signature or approval at his own cost and expense." The designer should, in calculating his costs on such a contract, make provision for the fee of the architect who reviews the plans and adds his stamp.

If the A.I.A. forms are used, the designer should make it clear (as stated) that he is not a registered architect and that one will be needed (if this is necessary) before the plans can be executed.

Working on Speculation

Designers, particularly young designers, often run across prospective clients who say, "Give me a rough sketch of what you're going to do and I'll decide whether or not to hire you." This is, of course, an invitation to work on speculation. It should be declined.

It never pays a designer to show a prospective client what he intends to do. The client may like the idea and decide that his own staff can execute it in final form. The client may turn the design down in all honesty. But years later, the design may appear to the designer's regret. Perhaps it was dredged up innocently from the prospect's subconscious; perhaps an employee or supplier of the prospective client copied it, either innocently or deliberately.

Moreover, a designer who shows a design on speculation meets sales resistance from the client at its highest. If the prospect likes the design, he realizes it will cost him money. If he doesn't like it, he's "home free." If he likes something that the proposed design suggests, he may feel free to have an altered version of the design executed in his own plant, honestly believing that he is fully justified in doing so.

On the other hand, if he has paid for the submission of a design, his sales resistance is at its lowest. If he rejects it, the fee is money thrown away. The only way he can recoup that money is to accept the design or to suggest changes that will make the design acceptable to him. If such changes are possible, he will have the designer himself make them in order to protect his investment in the design fee.

For these reasons, I always warn students in my courses never to work on speculation. If they learn only one thing from me, I hope it is this warning. One year Buckminster Fuller came to lecture at Pratt Institute. He held the students transfixed during his talk, which was to have been from 3:00 to 4:00. It ended at 11:00 P.M. when the superintendent said that he was forced to close the auditorium and turn out the lights.

The next day my students questioned me: "You tell us never to work on speculation but Mr. Fuller said that if we wanted to design something, go ahead and do it whether or not we had a customer for it. Whom shall we believe?" I reminded my inquisitors that back in the 30's Mr. Fuller had felt the need to design an automobile. He spent, as I understand it, some $30,000 each on two prototypes of the Dymaxion car. The car has never gone into production. My reply was: "If you can afford to spend $40,000 (close to $100,000 today) on a good idea that may be still-born, follow Mr. Fuller's advice; if you have to make a living, follow mine."

Actually, there was no essential disagreement between Mr. Fuller's advice and my own. It is one thing to work on speculation for a client; it is another to work on speculation for oneself. It is in the nature of a designer to design. If most designers were not paid to design, they would undoubtedly pay others for the privilege. If a designer has a project he believes strongly should be carried out, he should carry it out within the limits of his means. But that is not giving away free samples of work

85

to prospective clients. Saarinen, Bertoia, and Platner come to my mind as designers who thought of designs, carried them out and offered them for sale when fully perfected. And all of these ventures were profitable.

The Residential Interior Designer

The decoration of a home (or a room in a home) may be the most troublesome agreement for the decorator or designer to make. Part of this problem is due to the irregular way in which many interior designers are paid.

In most professions, the fee of the person retained is paid by his client and is commensurate with the time and work involved, the importance of the job, the skill of the professional, etc. Interior design is one of the few areas where the professional is paid not by his client but by his client's supplier. This is the case, of course, when the decorator keeps all or part of the decorator's discount.

There are other fields that follow the same practice. Advertising agencies (which used to be sales agencies for space in magazines) are still paid largely by the 15% commission they receive, not from their client, but from their client's source of space—the media. Travel offices likewise are paid not by their client but by the carrier or hotel with whom the client is dealing.

In the advertising field, the practice is slowly changing and some agencies pass the commission on to their clients and make a charge for their services.

The chief fault to the system as regards the residential interior designer is that the furniture showroom is shrouded in sham. A client enters with his decorator and is quoted a price of, perhaps, $1,000 for a sofa. The client does some mental arithmetic and says to himself, "That means $600." Even where the manufacturer quotes (as some do now) net prices, the question remains whether this is *net* net or just a spurious net, or a decorators' net (which is not quite as net as the price to a retailer). The impression that this arrangement leaves is that the designer (substitute "decorator") makes very little contribution to the client short of getting him a discount. This leads to the 10 percenter and similar evils.

Not the least of the faults of this arrangement is that it creates a conflict of interest (more apparent than real) between the client and the decorator. If the designer can specify a floor covering at $2 a square yard, he is paid only $\frac{1}{10}$ of what he would get if he specified one at $20 a square yard. While no honest decorator should be swayed by such facts in making his esthetic decision, it is not a wholesome arrangement. It is somewhat ameliorated by the fact that the designer is given a budget, and usually spends all of it, applying whatever is saved on one item to enriching another, so that his all-over income from the job is the same.

But if a designer-decorator is a professional, he should be paid like one. His fee (whether or not it is determined as a fraction of the budget) should be based on his services and not on the value of what he buys for the client. Many a designer can tell you that it is often more work to select the color of a 9' × 12' rug for a residential job than to pick out thousands of square yards for a contract project.

The flat fee contract (either long form or letter) set forth at the end of this chapter is easily adaptable to a decorating or residential interior design job by inserting the project description in the appropriate place.

Not a General Contractor

The decorator should be careful to make it clear in any contract that his role is to specify the job and recommend suppliers and contractors, but that he is not a general contractor. He does not warrant the quality or workmanship of any goods bought or any work done on the job. These are the responsibilities of the suppliers or the trades. An appropriate clause to cover this exception follows:

> *The Designer will use his best efforts to recommend sources of supply and contractors to furnish the goods or do the work pursuant to this contract, but undertakes no obligation in connection therewith (except, when applicable to supervise the installation and approve the quality of any materials furnished to the client).*

It should also be made clear that the client rather than the designer is pledging his credit. Since most manufacturers will insist on billing the decorator (because they do not know the client), the decorator should also have an agreement that:

> *The client will pay all bills of suppliers and contractors within 10 days of submission and will, in case of any dispute, hold the Designer harmless from any claim by any supplier or contractor.*

Such a clause will (so long as the client is solvent) avoid an occurrence in which the client refuses to pay because he claims the work or material is defective and the designer is called upon to make good. If a clause such as the one recommended is in effect, it will be easier for the designer to tell the client and the supplier to fight it out between themselves.

Interior designers also find themselves in trouble because they agreed that a job would not exceed a certain budget. They should rather express as an agreement to "use their best efforts" to meet the budget. Very often the client's own wishes make him exceed the budget. A client of mine once agreed to design a restaurant (lock, stock and barrel—including furnishings, dishes, silverware, uniforms, etc.) within a certain price. As the design progressed (to the complete satisfaction of the client) the client started to trade up. He wanted better dishes, better chandeliers, etc. But when the budget was exceeded, he protested. For this reason, the designer's agreement in relation to budget should be expressed as an aim rather than a promise, unless he is given absolute discretion without requiring the client's approval, and he knows that prices will remain stable between the time of signing the contract and completing the job.

Form: Standard Contract for Consultation Agreement

Dear _____;

    In accordance with our verbal understanding, we are writing to confirm the basis upon which we propose to consult with you in regard to _____

    I will confer with you and your staff at _____ _____, on _____, with a view to suggesting improvements in the style, design, and marketability of your _____

    Within _____ of our conferences, I will submit to you a report of our conference, together with my recommendations.

    You agree to pay me at the rate of _____ dollars ($) per day for this consultation and for the preparation of my report, but it is understood that in no event will the charges for my services exceed _____ dollars ($). In addition, you will reimburse me at actual cost for expenses in connection with my services, such as traveling, blue prints, telephone tolls, and _____

    If the above is satisfactory to you, please sign the enclosed copy of this letter, as indicated below, and return to me.

Yours etc.

AGREED TO:

_____, 19 _____

_____

By _____

Title

Part IV:
Royalties and Patents

The Royalty Agreement

The chief advantage of a royalty contract—to the designer at least—is that, should the design be successful it is more profitable than any other form of remuneration. One of the most successful designs for dinnerware returned its designer more than a million dollars in royalties. On a flat fee or straight-time basis, the designer would have been lucky to receive two or three thousand dollars for the design. But on the royalty basis, the manufacturer felt that he was passing the cost on to the consumer and was delighted to pay the larger sum of the royalty for the continuing sales of his line over the years.

Another advantage of the royalty arrangement is that it permits the designer to retain some control over the way his designs are carried out. When a design is sold, i.e., if the designer is compensated for it either on a time or flat-fee basis and that is his total compensation, the manufacturer feels that the designer's connection with the design is ended. Unless the designer's name is to be used in conjunction with the sale of the product (in which case the product must conform reasonably to the original), the manufacturer can make any changes he deems advisable. In Robsjohn-Gibbings' words, a manufacturer could "paint a moustache on the Mona Lisa" once he had bought and paid for it. However, when the designer is to be paid by a royalty, he has a continuing interest in the design, and the client will usually give him the right (whether or not the designer's name appears in connection with the finished product) to insist that the goods as sold conform to the approved sample.

To the extent that he is interested in some psychic return for his work, the royalty agreement gives the designer the satisfaction of knowing that the designs are going to be presented in the approximate form in which he finished them. To the extent that he is interested in the financial return, the designer will know that he is gambling (and a royalty agreement is a gamble) on his designs as conceived and carried out— and not on some product aborted from his original concept.

In order to keep the royalties coming in, the designer is usually willing to refresh and refurbish designs on which he is receiving royalties without additional charge or with only a nominal charge. This further reduces costs to the manufacturer—and helps him to continue making money by keeping the line new and saleable.

The real virtue of a royalty agreement, of course, is that it is possible to obtain big money in the long run. Naturally, if a design is unsuccessful, the remuneration will be small; but when it is successful, the royalty payments may far exceed any payment for the sale of a design for a lump sum. While it is true that the consumer must pay whatever fee the designer receives, in whatever form, the royalty arrangement enables the manufacturer to calculate it in the price by a simple matter of arithmetic. If the royalty is five percent, then five percent is added to the cost. If the flat fee is, say, $1000, the manufacturer doesn't know whether to charge each piece with $1 of design cost (on the theory that he would sell 1000 units) or $5 (on the theory that he would sell 200 units). In a royalty deal, on the other hand, the manufacturer must amortize only the advance, usually so low that it can be recovered from royalties on the minimum expected sale.

How much Royalty?

It is often difficult to determine in advance what rate of royalty should be paid. The norm in most agreements is five percent, that is, five percent of the price actually received by the client (after deducting allowances, rebates, refunds, such items as packing and freight when they are billed separately, and sales taxes), but the five percent figure is far from universal. In the publishing field, authors of text books normally receive six percent, while authors of so-called trade books receive royalties that start at ten percent (of the retail price) and accelerate rapidly as the sales volume increases. However, this is due to the peculiar economics of the publishing industry. After the cost of typesetting and engravings is amortized over the first few thousand books, the cost of additional copies goes down rapidly (and the publisher's gross profit goes up rapidly) so that larger royalties can soon be paid.

In general, the royalty agreed upon is, to use the mathematical phrase, a function of the expected volume. If a small sale at high price is contemplated, a high rate of royalty will be given. If, on the other hand, the designer and manufacturer contemplate a low price and a mass market, both parties will be well advised to reduce the royalty rate to 3 percent, or even lower. What is lost by reducing the return on each item is gained by the increase in the number of items sold. As one client remarked while examining his royalty statement, one percent of $1 million in sales is a lot more than ten percent of a $1000 of sales. Some manufacturers will pay royalties at two different rates on products from the same factory: such as five percent on the high-quality exclusive line and three percent on the mass-market line. Royalties may go down as low as (or lower than) one percent on, for example, asbestos-siding or low-end floor coverings. The contemplated volume of such products is so great that even a low rate will generate a large total royalty.

Royalty statements are delivered monthly or quarterly, depending on the bookkeeping system of the manufacturer. Permission is usually given the designer to examine the relevant records of the manufacturer in order to check on his royalties. This privilege is very rarely used, but its existence tends to guarantee that the manufacturer will be careful in calculating the royalties. It is not important whether the royalties are paid monthly or quarterly, but it is important that exact dates are set for the payments, so that the designer (and his client as well) can know when payments are due.

Some manufacturers will try to provide that the rate of royalties decreases after a certain volume is reached. This is hardly logical. As the volume increases, the manufacturer's profit increases (at a faster rate than the increase in sales) and, if anything, royalty rates should go up with volume.

One manufacturer often suggests that royalties stop altogether when they have reached a certain limit. There is certainly no justification for this. The practice goes back to the days of the founder who said, "I believe that designers get too lazy if they make too much money." The first time this ploy was tried on me, I answered: "I agree. But I also feel that manufacturers become lazy if they make too much money. I'll agree to a ceiling on royalties if you'll agree that after you reach an agreed-upon ceiling on your profits for the design, you'll sell the product at cost." Needless to say, no such agreement was forthcoming.

Certain manufacturers, who are used to dealing with inventions and patented products, try to provide that royalties stop when a competitor copies the design and cannot be prevented from doing so. This goes back to the practice in patented devices where royalties stop if the patent is declared invalid. The designer should make no such arrangement. Some of the most successful designs in the history of industrial design were never patented. The manufacturer often asks, "Do you mean that I must pay a royalty when my competitors can knock off the design without any payment?" The answer is that it is always cheaper to be a thief than an honest man. The manufacturer who pays royalties gets several advantages in return: he and only he can use the designer's name on the product if the marketing were properly handled; he is the originator and has the prestige as such to the trade and to the world at large. Further, he has the cooperation of the designer who can refresh, refurbish and redesign the product and still keep it a step ahead of the competitor's. Finally, I will always recommend that the designer agree—if the product is copied, and the copying cannot be stopped, and the price must be cut—to a cut in the rate of the royalty (the gross royalty already being cut by the reduction in price) to enable the manufacturer to keep his competitive position. In scores of contracts that contain such a provision, I have run across no manufacturer yet who has had to enforce it.

Discounts and Inflation

Some manufacturers prefer to pay a royalty of so much per piece rather than a percentage. They argue, "We sell at many different price levels, depending on such variables as the finish, the classification of customer, etc., that we would rather pay a flat royalty." In theory, there is nothing wrong with this; in practice it can cost the designer money. For instance, one manufacturer who sells his product at a discount ranging from 33-1/3 percent up to 50 percent wanted to calculate the royalty as though *all* items were sold at a discount of 50 percent and

10 percent. The designer wisely preferred to have him keep track of each sale. Another danger in this arrangement is our particularly inflated economy. If a product that sells at $100 rises in price to $120, the designer who gets a percentage of the sales prices keeps apace with the inflated dollar, while the one who gets a flat amount on each item receives a smaller and smaller percentage of the sale price. His income, in real money, is shrinking as fast as the dollar.

It may also happen that a designer comes up with a new and original approach, perhaps one that he can persuade the client to adopt only with great difficulty. If the approach should prove to be successful, the manufacturer may feel that he now "owns the idea" and may attempt to apply it to other items in the line without using the services of the designer. As a result, the other items will compete for sales with those on which the designer is receiving royalties. This situation is covered by the "copies and imitation" clause, which provides in effect that royalties are payable not only on the designer's original design, but also on any copy or imitation, or any product that uses any distinctive feature of his design. Though this clause has been used hundreds of times, I know of no situation in which it has been brought into effect, because the manufacturer, knowing of its existence, reasons that he'll have to pay the designer royalties on a copy, so he may as well call in the designer to design the copy himself.

Advances

It is customary to pay the designer an advance on his royalties. This enables him to keep up his cash flow until royalties come in. How large an advance? It should be small enough to insure the manufacturer that he will get it back in less than a year. Normally, it is the amount of royalties that would be earned as a minimum on the first six months' sales. Some companies, instead of withholding all royalties until the advances

have been wiped out, pay half royalties until the amount withheld equals the advances. This is a better deal for the designer
because he starts getting some money as soon as the first item
is sold, instead of going through the instability of fat years
and lean years.

Of course, the designer is no richer or poorer at the end of
the year whether or not he has received an advance, because
the advance will gradually be wiped out by deduction from
royalties. But his budgeting will certainly have been easier
and, moreover, he has had an expression of interest from the
manufacturer. If there is no advance, the designer may put in
a great deal of work and the product (for reasons having nothing to do with the design) may never be made. If, on the other
hand, the manufacturer has already paid an advance, he is
much more likely to try to recoup the advance by going into
production than he is to wipe it off as a loss.

Exclusivity

The exclusivity clause 2, (b) of the form at the end of this
chapter, should be very carefully drawn. Of course, the designer would be foolish to compete with himself by designing
a product for someone else that cuts into the market of the
product on which he is receiving royalties. But he may (and
should be able to) design other products in the same or similar
fields which are not competitive with the first item.

This is an era of conglomerate companies—for instance, Litton Industries controls furniture manufacturers, interior designers, office equipment manufacturers, etc. It would be
suicidal for a designer to agree (unless he were very well compensated) to design nothing for a competitor of one of these
conglomerates. He should give as wide an exclusivity as is
needed to protect his client, but no more.

The royalty agreement can bring revenue to a designer over
a period of years. It is a fortunate designer who has several

royalty agreements in force, each paying him an income. He is relieved of the pressing necessity of finding work to meet that week's payroll or that month's rent, and can take his time in selecting work or the area in which he wishes to develop. Despite this rosy position, a client once told me that the best advice I ever gave him was, "The time to look for work is when you have it; it's too late if you wait until you need it."

The one danger in a royalty contract is that, for reasons completely foreign to the design, the product may not sell or may not even reach the market. In the first royalty situation I ever handled, my client had designed a line which booked a great deal of business. But before any orders were filled the manufacturer went into bankruptcy. Months passed before we found a new manufacturer and royalties started to come in, and only for good fortune did the line survive at all. This risk of loss is minimal when the designer is selective about accepting a client.

One final twist: occasionally a designer will create a specialized design for a particular job, only to find that the item has a market outside of the client's needs. This is often discovered accidentally, when the manufacturers' source of supply sells the designs to the public without paying the designer. One very prominent office got around this situation by sending out invitations to bid on furniture made for its client. They required the successful bidder to make the line and offer it for sale to the public, paying the design firm a royalty. Royalties were waived on sales to the designer's original client. This had the advantage of reducing the cost to the client by getting him prices that were based on national sales rather than on a custom job. It also gave the designer an extra profit that might be forthcoming from royalties on national sales. In this case, I had suggested that the designer charge royalties even on sales to his client and refund the royalties to the client, since I believed that this would have been the more dramatic gesture and would have made the savings particularly apparent to the client. But the designer rejected this suggestion in favor of merely waiving royalties on sales to his original client. Needless to say, the entire arrangement was disclosed to the client, who gave permission for sale of the designs in the national market.

The Royalty Contract

The only form of arrangement for which I think the long form contract is more suitable than the letter of agreement is the royalty agreement. Many such agreements are embodied in letters, but the arrangement usually contains so many details that I feel the regular long form is more desirable.

The cautions mentioned in connection with other contracts (about limiting the area of exclusivity, protecting the use of the designer's name, etc.), apply with equal strength to the royalty agreement.

If the royalty agreement (or any other type of agreement) can be expressed in terms of a license from the designer to the client to manufacture an article which is patented by the designer (without regard to the validity of the patent), the designer's income from the agreement will, because of a special section of the Internal Revenue Code, be taxed at capital gain rates instead of as ordinary income. If these rates are in effect, the designer's income under the contract will be taxed at $\frac{1}{2}$ of his usual rate of 25%, whichever is lower.

Form: Standard Contract for Royalty Agreement

AGREEMENT BETWEEN _____

AND _____

THIS AGREEMENT, made as of the _____

day of _____ 19 _____, by and between _____

_____

_____ of _____

_____ (hereinafter called the "Designer")

and _____

of _____ (hereinafter called the "Client"),

WITNESSETH:

WHEREAS, _____

is a professional designer and a member in good standing of the
Industrial Designers Society of America and engaged in the field
of industrial design; and

WHEREAS, the Client desires to obtain the Designer's services in
designing certain products, and the exclusive right to his services
in the field of _____

NOW, THEREFORE, in consideration of the mutual promises, covenants and undertakings herein contained, the parties agree as
follows:

1. SERVICES:

The Client hereby engages the Designer's services to design _____

_____

to be manufactured, distributed and sold by the Client or for its
account. Said designs are hereinafter referred to as the "designs,"
and the products embodying the designs as the "product" or
"products." The Designer shall commence work on the designing
of said product on or before _____

and shall submit each design with a space provided on the reverse
side thereof for the Client's acceptance or rejection, and the Client
shall signify its acceptance or rejection of each design within
_____ of the receipt of same by signing in the space
provided therefor, and immediately returning rejected designs to
the Designer. All designs not returned within the period limited

101

shall be deemed accepted by the Client. If all designs are rejected, the Designer shall within _____ submit additional designs. The Client shall have no rights in connection with any rejected designs.

In connection with the design of said products, the designer further agrees:

(a) to confer with any representatives designated by the Client with respect to the type of merchandise required for manufacture and the price range desired:

(b) to make trips to the Client's factory, when mutually considered necessary and reasonable, to study limitations of production methods;

(c) at the request of the Client, to submit various designs as described above for said products, such designs to be presented on or before _____ in the form of _____;

(d) after the selection of designs for production by the Client, and notification thereof to the Designer, sufficiently to complete the designs selected and deliver to the Client within _____ weeks, said designs, in the form of _____;

(e) to work with the Client in developing final designs for said products, and promptly supervise and criticize models or samples in order that corrections may be made before full scale manufacture is undertaken;

(f) when requested by the Client, to consult on matters pertaining to the packaging and display of said designs;

(g) to consult with the Client or its agency and criticize (but not design) the art work, layouts and copy for promotional material, such as flyers, advertisements, and advertisement mats, in connection with the products manufactured from said designs.

In order to expedite the designing of said products, the Client will cooperate with the Designer and will supply the Designer and his assistants at all times with all technical data necessary to the effective performance of the Designer's services, and to acquaint the Designer with all previous or current developments or designing work on the problems submitted to him. The Designer agrees that all information received from the Client will be treated as confidential and not divulged.

2. EXCLUSIVE LICENSE:

The Designer hereby gives and grants to the Client, and the Client hereby accepts from the Designer, all upon the terms and conditions herein set forth, the sole and exclusive right, license, and privilege:

    (a) to manufacture, sell, and distribute, in domestic and foreign markets, products embodying the designs to be furnished to it by the Designer hereunder;

    (b) to reserve the exclusive use of the Designer's services in the field of _____ for the period from _____ to _____ and the Designer agrees that during the period he will not design such products for manufacture by any other than the Client. However, nothing contained in this paragraph shall prevent the Designer from designing for other manufacturers _____ _____;

    (c) to use the Designer's name in the marketing, sale, and distribution of said products, subject to the following restrictions:

        (1) Such name may be so used only after the Designer has given written approval of the manner in which the designs and finishes have been executed.

        (2) As each factory sample is received, the Designer will promptly criticize or approve it in writing.

        (3) If, in the opinion of the Designer, the appearance of any products as manufactured in regular production is not equivalent to that contained in the standard samples as approved by the Designer, the Designer may, in writing, call for the removal of his name from the article and the Client shall not use the Designer's name in connection therewith until the appearance again meets

with the Designer's approval.

(4) The Client agrees to submit the copy and art work for all such advertisements and promotional literature to the Designer for his approval before the final printing or issuance thereof.

3. COPIES AND IMITATIONS:

(a) The Client agrees, during the life of this contract, or at any time thereafter, not to copy or imitate, or to authorize the imitation or copying of, the designs submitted to the Client by the Designer, or any distinctive feature of the designs submitted to the Client by the Designer. Full royalties shall accrue on items which include any such distinctive feature, produced or sold by the Client, whether from designs furnished by the Designer or not. This shall not apply to any items in the form in which they are being produced by the Client at the time of signing this contract. If the Designer feels that any new pattern manufactured by the Client is similar to, or an imitation of, any designs submitted to the Client by the Designer, or any distinctive feature thereof, he will give the Client immediate notice thereof. Any dispute arising under this paragraph at any time shall be settled by arbitration, in accordance with Paragraph 12 hereof.

(b) The Client agrees that, if he subcontracts or purchases any part of the product from other sources, the Client will, upon the Designer's request, secure from the source of supply a written agreement that the source of supply will not make or offer any parts embodying distinctive features of the Designer's design, or employ any distinctive method or materials suggested by the Designer, either for the source's own account, or for any other manufacturer or distributor.

4. REMUNERATION:

(a) The Client agrees to pay the Designer, his heirs, or successors, a royalty of _____ per cent (____%) on all net billings paid by purchasers (less returns and discounts, but not discounts to purchasers who

are affiliated with the Client) of all products embodying the Designer's designs. The Client further agrees that for retaining the exclusive service and use of the name "_____" for the period as provided herein, it will pay the Designer a minimum guarantee of _____ dollars ($_____), such guarantee to be paid in the first instance by paying the Designer on a time basis for the Designer's designing and development costs for the furnishing of said designs. The Designer shall, at the end of each month, furnish the Client with a statement, with appropriate segregation of the services rendered, of the time devoted to each part of the design project by the Designer and his assistants respectively, during the preceding month, showing his or their respective rates. It is understood that these rates will consist of the actual rates, plus overhead and profit, and that, figured thus, the rates will be _____
_____.

The Client will pay for the time so billed within _____ weeks of receipt of each statement. The Designer agrees not to bill the Client for more than _____ dollars ($_____) on a time basis for his services during the first twelve (12) months, although the Designer's time for such work may run over the stipulated amount during said twelve (12) month period. The Client will pay, on the bill for the twelfth month, the amount necessary to bring the total to the amount of the aforesaid guarantee.

(b) It is understood that all monies paid by the Client for such time rates shall be applied against royalties accruing from _____ to _____, and further royalties will not be due or payable during said period until they exceed the amounts paid for time rates.

(c) Payments of royalties shall be made by the Client to the Designer, his heirs, or successors, on or before _____ _____ of each year following the first marketing of said products by the Client, in each case payment to include all royalties earned during the preceding _____

_____. Such payment shall be accompanied by a statement showing the shipments made by the Client, its agent, and representatives during the preceeding _____ _____. The Designer shall have the right to inspect and audit the relevant records of the Client, through an agent or attorney authorized by him. Payment of royalties shall continue so long as the products are manufactured and sold by the Client or by others, upon its order.

[Alternate for Paragraph 4, (a) (b)]

4. REMUNERATION:

(a) The Client agrees to pay the Designer, his heirs, or successors, a royalty of _____ per cent (____%) on all net billings paid by purchasers (less returns and discounts, but not discounts to purchasers which are affiliated with the Client) of all products embodying the Designer's designs. The Client further agrees that for retaining the exclusive services and use of the name "_____" for the period as provided herein, it will pay the Designer a minimum guarantee of _____ dollars ($_____), such guarantee to be paid in _____ equal installments beginning on _____.

(b) It is understood that all monies paid by the Client on account of the stated guarantee shall be applied against royalties accruing during the first year for which they are paid, and further royalties will not be due or payable during said fiscal year until royalties earned exceed the amount paid on account of said guarantee.

5. TRAVEL AND INCIDENTAL EXPENSES:

Extra blueprints, all long distance telephone charges, traveling costs, and expenses incidental thereto, shall be billed to the Client as extras; but shall be billed at actual costs, with no added percentage for overhead or profit, such expenses not to be applied against any royalties paid. Travel costs and expenses will be incurred only when and to the extent that they have been authorized by the Client. The Designer will keep long distance charges to a reasonable amount.

6. OPTION OF RENEWAL:

If the Client wishes to continue to receive the exclusive services of the Designer in this field, as defined herein, it may do so by informing him on or before _____ of any year in which this contract is in effect, beginning with the year 19_____, that this exclusivity is desired; and by guaranteeing that beginning _____ of said year, and for a period of twelve (12) months thereafter, the Designer's royalties will amount to at least _____ dollars ($_____), payment of which shall be made by the Client to the Designer on or before _____ of the year for which the option is exercised. If either

(a) such written notice and guarantee are not received by the Designer on or before _____ of any year, or

(b) the guaranteed payment is not made by the Client upon the due date, then and in either event, the Designer will be free to design the products covered by this agreement for others.

If, in any year during which the Client exercises this option to retain the Designer's exclusive services, the Client so requests, the Designer will submit _____ additional designs for the products in addition to the submission of said designs as set forth in Paragraph 1 hereof.

7. RIGHTS IN THE DESIGNS:

(a) The designs submitted by the Designer for said products shall be and remain the property of the Designer, together with any and all drawings, models, and samples furnished by the Designer, subject to the exclusive right to manufacture, sell, and distribute the accepted designs herein granted to the Client, so long as the Client is not in default of its obligations under this contract, _____ shall have the right to possession of all designs and models.

(b) The Client shall have the right to have the designs or any one of them copyrighted or patented with the Government of the United States in the Designer's name, but at the Client's expense; and the Designer shall give the Client every cooperation necessary and desirable in order to enable it to procure such copyright or patent. The Designer agrees to license the Client during the term of this agreement, or so long as the Client is not in default in payment of royalties, to use the designs covered by such patent or copyright.

(c) If such designs or processes or any of them shall be copyrighted or patented, the Client may at its option sue to enforce or protect said copyright or patent, and in such event the Designer agrees to join in or bring such action for damages or injunction as the Client may direct, the Client at all times to hold the Designer free and harmless from costs and expenses in connection with same. In all such events, the Designer will employ such counsel as the Client may direct, and all recoveries shall be received by the Designer for the Client's benefit and turned over to the Client except that the portion of the recovery representing royalty shall be retained by, or paid to, the Designer, his heirs, or successors.

8. TERMINATION:

(a) Should accepted designs not be produced and marketed by the Client within _____ of the date hereof, possession of the designs shall be returned to the Designer, the license to manufacture same shall terminate, and the Designer shall have the right to make any use whatsoever of such designs. The termination of the license under this clause shall not terminate the obligation of the Client to pay any amounts due or to become due under contract.

(b) In the event that the manufacture of said products is prevented, hindered, or delayed by strikes, fires, floods, or by any similar circumstances beyond the control of the Client, the periods of limitation provided herein for the commencement of manufacture of said products shall be extended by the time during which the manufacture of said products is so prevented, hindered, or delayed.

(c) In the event that the manufacture of said products is prevented because of war, government restrictions, or any other similar circumstances beyond the control of the Client, the Client may, at its option, terminate this agreement by returning the designs to the Designer and paying to the Designer the amount due for work already performed hereunder, plus _____ dollars ($_____) for the Designer's creative work and his expense of changing over to other work.

9. MODIFICATION OR CHANGE OF AGREEMENT:

This agreement is the entire understanding between the parties, and no modification or change in this agreement shall be effective unless in writing and executed by both parties hereto.

10. INSOLVENCY:

Should the Client be liquidated or become bankrupt or insolvent, or be reorganized under Chapter X or any other provision of the Bankruptcy Act, right to the use of the Designer's designs cannot be sold unless they are subject to all provisions of this agreement.

11. ASSIGNMENT OF CONTRACT:

This agreement shall not be assigned by either party without the written consent of the other, but in the event of either party being succeeded by another by the operation of law, this contract shall be binding upon and inure to the benefit of such successor. The Designer may assign royalties due to him under this contract by written notice to the Client.

12. ARBITRATION:

Any and all disputes and controversies arising hereunder or in connection herewith shall be submitted to the American Arbitration Association for arbitration, pursuant to the rules and regulations of that body then obtaining. The cost of arbitration shall be borne equally by both parties and the decision of the arbitrator shall be binding and conclusive upon them.

13. ADDITIONAL TERMS:

_____

IN WITNESS WHEREOF, the parties hereto have executed this agreement on the _____ day of nineteen hundred and _____

_____

Designer

_____

Client

Part V:

Inventions and Disclosures

Shops Rights

If a designer conceives of a design or invention while working for someone else, and working in the field to which the invention is pertinent, to whom does it belong?

This question is a part of the general problem known to lawyers as "shop rights," and does not differ from the same situation arising outside the field of design.

If an employee conceives an idea in a field other than that in which he is employed, his employer obviously has no rights to his invention (except in rare cases where they have a specific agreement to the contrary). Should a bookkeeper for an automobile company, who has no duties other than keeping books, invent a new carburetor, the invention is his and his employer can claim no right to it.

But if an employee was hired to work in a given area—to parallel the case mentioned, if he was hired to work on carburetor systems, though the invention is still his, the employer has the right to a free, non-exclusive license to use the design, providing it was made on company time. While the patent would be issued in the name of the inventor (as it always is), the employer is entitled to the use of the design without payment under the "Shops Rights" rule. The employee could, nevertheless, license its use to others for a charge.

In a large business, it is often difficult to separate the contributions of individual employees working on a project or conceiving an invention. Because these are joint efforts, to define the contribution of a single employee would be like trying to unravel a tangled web. For this reason (and also to prevent the limitation of the employer's rights to those granted under the shops rights rule), employers often require that employees sign agreements limiting their inventions or disclosures as a condition of employment. Briefly, this agreement 1) stipulates that the employee convey or agree to convey to the employer all rights to any inventions or discoveries which the employee conceives while employed by the company, and 2) requires the employee to treat as confidential any information, knowledge of techniques, trade secrets or other information disclosed in the course of the worker's employment with that company.

The first proviso of the contract for Inventions and Disclosures that follows this chapter is of little practical value if the invention involved is valuable enough for the employee to quit his job in order to exploit it. It is very difficult, except in the case of a team effort in a large office, to prove that someone conceived an invention on company time. If a worker is cagey, it is easy enough for him to keep his invention or discovery secret, quit his job, and disclose the invention as a new idea at a later date. It is questionable whether an agreement would be valid if it required the employee to turn over to the company inventions he made *after* he left the company's employ.

Where the invention is so small that it would not pay the worker to give up his job to exploit it, the occasion to hide it does not arise. By and large it pays an employer to secure such

113

agreements since it may prove valuable to him at some future date.

The disclosure agreement, which turns the rights of an invention over to the employer, is most successful when coupled with a suggestion program. This compensates employees for making valuable suggestions. While it encourages employees to disclose their new ideas, it does not give them the feeling that they are being bought lock, stock and barrel.

Disclosing Company Secrets

The agreement not to disclose confidential information presents more difficulty. Employers are apt to treat *all* information disclosed to workers as secret and confidential. It is *not* possible to keep a worker from using everything he has learned in the course of his experience. His increase in skill, his knowledge of which techniques his employer uses (so long as these are not secret techniques), the names of his customers (so long as he doesn't physically copy customer lists), and similar information may be used by the worker independently or on his new job. But if the employer has a genuinely secret formula or technique, the worker may not disclose it, particularly if he has agreed not to.

Here again, breach by the employee is difficult to prove. Very rarely does the case arise where it can be shown that a worker carried a secret from one employer to another. More often, there was a seepage, rather than a full-scale leak. A worker told someone else in the business, who told a third party, who told a fourth—and the secret is out. Nevertheless, it is wise for the employer to obtain a non-disclosure agreement. It certainly guards against an employee who decides he will peddle his company's secrets directly to a competitor.

In reality, the possibility of a worker's coming up with a new invention, or peddling company secrets is fairly remote, while the worker's ability to circumvent the agreements is strong.

Yet, employers may wish to secure whatever protection such an agreement can give them. Unfortunately, however, the employer often goes about it in a way that causes resentment to the new employee. He has a lawyer prepare a contract form in legalese to be signed by the new employee. It appears to tie him up tighter than the proverbial drum. No explanation is given the employee; he is presented with this formidable document and told to sign. As a matter of good employee relations, the document submitted to the worker can be just as effective and binding if it has a gentler, more colloquial tone. Examples of both types of documents follow this chapter.

Form: Agreement re. Inventions and Disclosures

Agreement made as of the _____ day of _____ 19____, by and between EXCELSIOR DESIGNERS, Inc., a corporation duly organized under the laws of the State of New York, and having its principal office at _____, hereinafter called "the Corporation" and _____ of _____, hereinafter called "the Employee":

WITNESSETH:

WHEREAS, the Employee is [has been] employed by the Corporation in a confidential capacity and for the purpose, among others, of conceiving ideas, inventions and plans, and making discoveries which may be used in the business of the Corporation, and

WHEREAS, the Corporation has made the agreement of the Employee to the conditions hereinafter stated a condition of [continued] employment of the Employee,

NOW, THEREFORE, in consideration of the [continued] employment of the Employee by the Corporation, the parties agree as follows:

1. The Employee agrees that an idea, invention, discovery or conception which the Employee conceives or develops while in the employ of the Corporation shall be and become the sole property of the Corporation, and the Employee agrees that he will disclose same to the Corporation as conceived and that he will, at the Corporation's request and expense, execute any applications for patent, copyright or similar protection requested by the Corporation, together with assignments or exclusive licenses thereof.

2. The Employee agrees that the compensation he receives or shall receive as Employee of the Corporation shall cover any inventions, discoveries, processes or ideas he conceives or develops while in the employ of the Corporation and that he will not be entitled to any additional compensation therefor; if the Company decides, in its unlimited discretion to make any additional payment for such inventions, discoveries, processes or ideas, such payment, if any, shall not constitute an admission by the Corporation that the Employee is entitled to any payments in addition to his salary as Employee.

3. If, in the course of his employment, the Employee learns any

trade secrets, processes, formulas, procedures or ideas of the Corporation (including, without limitation, lists of customers, lists of resources, methods of operation, etc.), Employee agrees that he will treat such disclosures as confidential, and that he will not, during the period of his employment, or at any time thereafter, disclose such information (to any competitor of the Corporation or otherwise) without the consent, in writing, of the Corporation.

IN WITNESS WHEREOF, the parties hereto have executed this agreement on the date first above written.

EXCELSIOR DESIGNERS, Inc.

By _____

_____
Employee

Form: Letter Agreement re. Inventions and Disclosures

Dear John:

Welcome to the Excelsior team. We hope that you will be happy working with us, and are writing this letter to outline certain rules of our firm.

We want to encourage all of our fellow-workers to be as creative as possible. To this end, we disclose all of our methods of operation, resources, customers, techniques, etc. We also make whatever facilities are needed available to any co-worker who wants to develop any new ideas. Your section head is Mr. _____ and he will be glad to help you in obtaining any information or assistance you need.

Under these circumstances, we expect all members of our organization to agree that they will treat all disclosures as confidential and will not make such information available to anyone outside of our organization without written permission.

Likewise, we expect all of our workers to throw into the common pot any ideas, inventions, discoveries, etc., which they conceive, so that they become the property of the corporation and can, if necessary, be developed by and in collaboration with your co-workers. If any of your ideas is capable of patent or similar protection, we may ask you to execute (at our expense) the proper applications, and assignment of exclusive license to the Corporation. We have a policy of paying for such contributions to our joint effort, but the amount of the payment, or whether or not any payment should be made, is a matter of management determination.

You have probably already been told of our group insurance and hospitalization programs. If you have any questions about this coverage, talk to Mr. _____.

We are sending you this letter in duplicate. Please sign and return the carbon copy to show that you agree to its terms. The original is for your files.

Yours very truly,

Part VI:
The Negative Restrictive Covenant

The Fair Right to Work

The Negative Restrictive Covenant is simply a lawyer's name for an agreement that limits someone's right to work—either for a competitor or in the same general field.

An employer may be hesitant to have a worker assume responsibility for an important project or negotiate with clients lest he make it the occasion to leave the job, taking the clients or projects with him. Likewise, clients often disclose confidential information to their designers and want some assurance that this information will not leak or be leaked by the designer or his staff. Even the government recognizes the dangers inherent in this situation. It decrees that an ex-government employee cannot work on a project he was concerned with in the course of his employ for two years after he leaves the job. This keeps a revenue agent, for instance, from quitting and going to the taxpayer whose return he was auditing to solicit his business to "beat the rap."

In the Anglo-American legal doctrine, there is no way in which a court can require a worker to work for a specific employer. Even if there were, surveillance would be extremely difficult. How do you force a designer to design? How do you prove that he is not really giving the job everything he's got?

What is Fair?

But if an employee cannot be made to stay on the job, it can be made unprofitable for him to leave by getting him to agree that he won't do certain things—work for accounts he has serviced, go to a competitor in a certain area, etc. If the agreement is one that is essentially fair, the courts will enforce it. What is fair? Basically, an agreement that is broad enough to protect the employer's interests without putting the worker out of business. The first rule of thumb is that there must be a limitation on the restriction both as to field or area and as to time. A designer can't be required to commit economic suicide by agreeing that he will *never* work at his trade or profession *anywhere* in the world. An agreement that he won't open a studio across the street within three months of leaving the job is fair. Just where between these two extremes the dividing line falls is a question that varies with circumstances and from state to state. See a lawyer about how far you can go. Some states strike down the whole agreement if it is too broad, while others will enforce it to a lesser extent than is spelled out in words.

In some instances this restriction may be downright unfair to the employee. If the designer had no connection with a client while he was on the job, he should not be restricted from working for that client in the future. I have always advised an employee that if he hadn't worked directly on a client's account, he is free to take a job with a competitor who is currently handling that client, particularly if he himself had nothing to do with the client's switching and will not capitalize on a relationship with the client arising from his former employment. Nevertheless, some design firms have sought (unsuccessfully, so far) to prevent ex-employees from taking jobs with firms now servicing their former clients. Even were the restrictive covenant enforceable, it would accomplish little. It might make it more difficult temporarily for the competing firm to render service to the former client, though even this is doubtful. There are enough able designers unhampered by covenants to offer their talents and to complete a job. To enforce the negative restrictive covenant against an innocent designer is strictly unprofessional.

Aside from the morality of enforcing a restrictive covenant that overreaches, it is probably bad business and certainly it is bad employee relations to place onerous limits on the worker. A really good designer will not sign such an agreement unless he is desperate for work, and a firm probably wouldn't want to hire him under those conditions. If design is indeed an honorable profession, an employer should treat his employees as co-members of that profession and allow them (if they leave) to compete for business in the open market. The threat of losing business to a junior designer who seduces clients away is more imagined than real. The greater likelihood is that a competitor will get the account and try to hire the man who services it as extra insurance for retaining it.

Like the shops rights letter of the preceding section, the restrictive covenant can be spelled out in a formal contract or in a letter contract. The letter form is recommended as better employment policy.

Here is a suggested clause to be inserted into the formal contract:

> "As further consideration of his employment by the Employer, the Employee agrees that he will not, for two (2) years after the termination of his employment hereunder, perform or do any work directly or indirectly for any firm, person or corporation which has been a client of the Employer during Employee's employment, nor for any competitor of Employer who serves such any client."

THE NEGATIVE RESTRICTIVE COVENANT

Or this suggested paragraph can be used in an informal letter covering the situation:

> *"We hope, that as you become familiar with our method of operation, to introduce you to our clients and have you work directly with them on various jobs. In order to permit us to do so freely, we ask our co-workers to agree that they will not work for any such client, nor for any competitor serving such client, for a period of two years after leaving us."*

If the agreement will not be inserted into the contract, the letter form completing this section can be used. As a matter of good employee relations, this letter should be phrased as amicably as possible and should be only as broad as is fair to both parties.

Form: Letter for Negative Restrictive Covenant

To our employees:

It is our policy to permit our employees, when qualified, to work as closely as possible with our clients, and to contact them directly.

In the course of your employment with us, you may be made privy to confidential matters of our clients' business and to some of their trade secrets. Our clients require an undertaking from us (and from our employees) that they will not disclose any of this material offered in confidence.

We in turn, in order that we may feel free to give our employees the freest possible rein in working with our clients, require our employees to agree that they will not, directly or indirectly, serve any of our clients whose accounts they have worked on for a year after they leave our employ, and that they will not at any time divulge any confidential information received from us or from our clients.

We are writing this letter to you in duplicate. In order to show your agreement to these conditions of your employment, please sign and return the enclosed carbon copy.

We hope that your stay at this office will be a happy and fruitful one and will welcome any suggestions you may make that will improve our service to our clients.

Very truly yours,

_____

Signed.

AGREED TO:

_____ L. S.

Some Afterwords

How to Protect an Idea

The question I am asked most frequently and answer least satisfactorily is: How does someone protect an idea? Designers often have potentially profitable suggestions for business and industry and wish to present them to the right parties without having them stolen.

At the outset, I must make it clear that there is no way to protect a "naked" idea. It must be made concrete in some way, i.e., as a process or a product. The more concrete it is made, the easier it will be to protect.

Obviously, if the person approached with the idea agrees to pay for it in advance, the problem is half solved. But only half, because the law requires that the idea be original and unknown to the prospect. The landmark case explaining these conditions arose in New York in a suit called Soule v. Bon Ami. As we were taught the case in law school, the facts are:

The plaintiff, Louis Soule, approached the manufacturer of Bon Ami (A pre-white-tornado-type scouring powder) and said, "I have an idea that will enable you to make more money. If I tell you about it, will you give me half of all profit derived from using the idea? The manufacturer agreed. Whereupon Soule replied, "Charge more for your product. The spread between your wholesale and retail prices is greater than that of your competition."

Shortly thereafter the manufacturer raised his prices and Soule sued for his half of the increased profits. The case went to the New York Court of Appeals, the state's highest court, where the decision was made in favor of the defendant. "Everybody knows," the court reasoned, "that you make more money if you charge higher prices. You can't expect to be paid for such an obvious suggestion." The case still stands. A volunteer who offers to sell a suggestion must represent that it is novel. I say "volunteer" because, obviously, if the Bon Ami Company had hired Mr. Soule as a consultant to suggest ways to increase profits, he could collect even on an idea that was old hat.

On examination of the court's opinion, the case turns out to be more complex than appears from a casual reading. Soule was, in fact, an economist who specialized in pricing. He had made a careful study of the scouring powder market and had determined that Bon Ami could safely raise its price to the amount suggested without losing any sizable portion of its business. It is not necessarily obvious that you make more money by raising prices. A product can price itself out of the market and bring in *less* profit. But the case holds that no compensation need be given for an unsolicited idea, unless it is clearly new and unique.

Yet volunteers have collected for just such advice. An advertising man went to the Century Brewing Company suggesting that a good slogan would be "The Brew of the Century." Whether or not this slogan was already in the works (and it is hard to believe that the manufacturer would not have hit upon it independently) a court awarded the plaintiff damages when the company used the line. As one of the judges argued in a dissenting opinion, the man had suggested only a slight switch in the defendant's corporate name.

Even if the idea is new and unique, it is not sufficient to tell the prospect and then demand payment if it is subsequently used. He must agree to pay for it. One case that makes this point involved Fred Waring, the bandleader. Because radio and television programs are gluttonous consumers of material, each week the producers of Waring's weekly program were forced to think up new ideas. One day, an agent who packaged such shows suggested to Waring's agent that a series of programs be built around listener's requests for songs that had been influential in their lives—"our song," as the romantics say. Later

126

when the bandleader produced a program along those lines (he denied having heard the suggestion), the agent sued for payment. Though Waring was unable to disprove an agreement for payment, he relied on a custom in the industry. The court held that in the absence of an agreement (express or implied), a volunteer could not collect for a suggestion. In other words, at least two things must be present to recover: an idea that is new and original (or at least not known to the person to whom the suggestion is made) and an agreement to pay for it if used.

How does someone prove that he made the suggestion? Some people suggest that he write himself a registered letter outlining the suggestion and that when received, it be kept intact with the date stamped across the flap. When litigation arises (if it should) the letter is produced in court and opened with a flourish to show that it contains the very idea being litigated. This may be fine for a Perry Mason program, but it is not adequate for legal protection. In at least one case where it was tried, the issue became whether the envelope had been steamed open before trial and resealed. The basic issue was obscured in the shuffle.

The question in such cases is rarely whether or not the plaintiff had such an idea at a particular date. If proof of this were sufficient, someone could simply write the idea out, date it and have a friend witness it. The real issue usually revolves on: Was there a promise to pay for the idea if used? Did the person using the idea in fact get it from the plaintiff, or was it also available from other sources?

Should the person to whom the idea is to be submitted agree to pay for its use, the form to cover the situation is simple to devise:

Dear Mr. _____ .
I have conceived an idea that I believe would be valuable

127

to you. In consideration of disclosing this idea to you, you have agreed
(1) to treat the disclosure as confidential and not to disclose it to anyone else unless and until we have reached an agreement on my compensation for the idea.
(2) that you will pay me at least _____ dollars, or _____ percent of your profits for the use of the idea.
(3) to let me know within _____ days whether or not you wish to use the idea.
In order to show your agreement to these terms, please sign and return the enclosed copy of this letter.
Yours truly,
Agreed to: _____ .

Even though this seems to be a harmless form, experience shows that the possibility of getting it signed is practically zero. In fact, the average company will run like the Devil from such a letter, not because they do not want good suggestions but because they do not want law suits. As the Century Brewing Case indicates, a firm that listens to suggestions lays open to litigation if it ever adopts anything resembling the suggestion—even though the idea embodied is very obvious. It costs money to try law suits even when they are won. Moreover, juries are apt to sympathize with an individual claimant against the defendant, a big corporation. In their opinion, the defendant will not miss the small amount of the verdict.

The person who writes to a large organization offering to disclose an idea or making such a disclosure will probably get back a letter phrased like the following:

Dear Mr. _____:
Thank you for offering to make a suggestion to us. Our policy is to seek suggestions only from within our organization, or from our advertising agency. We are therefore returning your letter enclosed herein. If you wish us to consider your

suggestion, please sign and return the enclosed form. Thanks again for thinking of us. We are glad to know that you use our products.'

Very truly yours,

The enclosure will probably read something like this:

Dear XYZ Corp.:

I would like to suggest an idea to you. In consideration of the idea, I agree that my rights, if any, against you will be limited to those under the United States Patent laws, and that you are to be the sole and final judge of the originality of the idea and of its value. I further agree that in no event will I ever sue for more than $100 for the use of the suggested idea.

Yours very truly,

What course of action should the recipient of such a form letter take? I like to point out that if an idea is never disclosed to a prospect for fear of its being stolen it will accompany its originator to the grave. I consider it better business to gamble on disclosing it and *perhaps* having it stolen than never to disclose it at all. At least by so doing it may eventually pay off. By and large, companies do pay for ideas. They are glad to get them and happy to pay for profitable ones.

Overvaluation of Ideas

Because of the great fund of lore—all of it untrue—that has sprung up about suggestions, the average person has a misguided sense of what an idea is worth. A popular story tells of a man (the name depends upon who tells it) who approached George Washington Hill and said, "I have a slogan in my hand. If you use it I want $75,000 for it; if not, I'll tear it up." Hill asked to see it. The man read, "Be Happy—Go Lucky." And George Washington Hill sat down and wrote out a check for $75,000.

There's not a word of truth in the story. The slogan was

obtained by the American Tobacco Company without cost from its advertising agency (who profited, as usual, from the 15 percent commission it received on ads placed). A slogan is worth very little until thousands of dollars are spent making it into a "household word."

Another bit of folklore follows the same general outline as the Lucky Strike story, except that it is the owner of Coca-Cola who is approached. This time the paper has "Bottle it" written on it. Again, the man with the bright idea gets a check for $75,000. This tale is likewise untrue.

The reason for repeating these canards is that most companies dread a lawsuit arising from people who hear the stories and then have fantastic notions of what such ideas are worth (to say nothing of facing the jury who also believes them).

All people who make suggestions are not devious. But most believe that their ideas are new when in reality they are almost cliches. Every Christmas the Reynolds Tobacco people get scores of copies of the same suggestion: "Have a poster showing the star in the East and the three Wise Men riding on camels to visit the Christ Child. Underneath, the caption reads: 'In Days of Old, Camels carried Wise Men. Nowadays, Wise Men Carry Camels.'" The ad has never been used not only because it might be offensive to religious groups but also because its use would provoke hundreds of claimants who thought they had originated the idea.

Most businesses have adopted some method for brushing off suggestions with as little loss of good will as possible. Years ago, I worked for the law firm that represented Macy's. Macy's like Sears, General Motors and others, receives thousands of suggestions, one of the penalties for being a leader in the field. As part of our service to Macy's, we devised a *modus operandi* for handling suggestions. It included returning the original letter to the person who offered the suggestion. The following incident illustrates the pitfalls inherent in the most cautious system.

A customer wrote Macy's with a fantastic suggestion for selling coffee at lower prices against sales receipts from other purchases. In the absence of the advertising manager who handled such matters, his assistant sent the polite form letter that we had drafted and returned the customer's own letter. The person wrote again saying, "I have an even better idea than last time, etc." This letter reached the desk of the advertising manager, fresh from vacation. Thinking the letter a continuation of prior correspondence, he scribbled on it a note to his assistant: "What's this all about?" To which the assistant penciled the reply, "This guy is a nut." The letter was sent through the usual channels including its return to the sender. Unfortunately, no one erased the pencilled notes. In a few days, Macy's was threatened with a suit for libel because the customer had been called "a nut." The case never went to court, however, because the communication between two employees performing their common duties is considered privileged information.

Sell the Prospect with Care

Someone with a legitimate idea to sell should select his prospect with care. In the final analysis, the honesty of the prospect must be relied upon. I have always felt that the larger the firm, the safer—not because people in big businesses are more honest than those in small businesses, but because there is safety in size. An individual in business for himself can say that he had already considered an idea, or had known of it for a long time. He can even fake a back-dated file to prove it. There are too many people in a large corporation who would have to be corrupted to make a lie stand. There is always the risk that one person refuses to go along with the story or that a disgruntled or discharged employee may carry the tale to the person who made the suggestion.

Entree to the executive who makes the decisions on a suggestion can avoid the routine and required release. What worries the firm is not the professional who makes a sensible suggestion, but the layman who thinks that his idea is the greatest thing since bubble gum—and worth millions. At least once a week I am approached by designers who have a gadget they describe as "the greatest thing since the hula hoop." I am then required to point out that the man who designed the hula hoop (if, in fact, it was designed and didn't just happen) was not the one who made the money—the man who first merchandised it really cashed in.

I am sure that if either Raymond Loewy or George Nelson wrote to General Motors offering a suggestion, neither would get a form letter in reply. They would probably be invited to submit the sugegstion. To get professional treatment is to be half the way home.

The ideal situation is getting a prospect to invite suggestions from the designer. The suggestions then need not be unique or new. They may be whatever the designer considers the best choice of several known solutions. If Soule had been hired by Bon Ami as a market consultant and had suggested raising wholesale prices, he could have collected on his advice even though "everybody knows you make more money if you raise prices."

A company's form letter and release may be amended in favor of a designer with a personal introduction to someone in authority. But the top echelon must be reached. Whereas the subordinate is bound by and required to stick to standard office procedure, the head of the business can exercise his own discretion.

The idea that is capable of patent protection is the safest and surest from theft. Copyright, if available, protects only the form in which the idea is expressed but not the idea itself and explains why it is effective only for literary ideas and music. Even a patent protects only the way the idea is carried out, and reasonable variations of it, but not the basic idea itself. Ideas such as, "Bottle it," or methods of operation (like suggesting that a price be raised, or a program be based on "our song") can be protected neither by patent nor copyright.

Fundamentally, the rules for proferring a suggestion can be summed: 1) first get a written and dated record of the idea and make it as concrete as possible; 2) offer it to someone whom you believe you can trust (preferably someone to whom you have a personal introduction); and 3) offer it as a professional rather than as an amateur.

Patenting an Original Design

It is unwise to rush into patenting. Many amateur entrepreneurs have ended up with a drawerful of patents and no money. Patents are indicated only where there is a fair possibility of commercial exploitation. In fact, most contracts provide that patents be secured "at the request and expense" of a manufacturer.

A little known rule pertaining to patents is that application must be filed within one year of public disclosure of the invention. When a product is offered for sale, or even if its picture should be published in a magazine, the time has started to run. Unless the patent is applied for within the year, application will be rejected.

Inventions should be carefully considered before patent application is sought. By the time claims are allowed and rejected, the area of the patent could become very narrow. Patent attorneys are patent-minded; they almost always recommend a patent application. This is not because they are grasping or over-reaching but only because their training points them firmly in this direction. A doctor once pointed out to me that surgeons often recommend surgery not because they need (or want) the work, but because they are trained to consider surgery the ultimate weapon in the medical armory. A surgeon knows that an appendix once removed causes no trouble. Patent attorneys suffer from the same bias. And, as it is advisable to get an opinion from a non-surgeon about the necessity of surgery, it is not a bad idea to have someone other than a patent attorney advise on whether or not to secure a patent.

There are other considerations that may influence the decision to patent a product or design. Securing a patent (even an invalid one) may "keep the thieves away." Copiers are more reluctant to steal an item that is patented than one that is not. Even where a legal opinion would show the patent to be invalid, in many cases they will refrain from copying rather than chance litigation—even successful litigation. Patent lawyers refer to this as the "deterrent" value of patents. I have also heard it referred to as "blackmail value."

A patent, even though weak, may be desirable for tax relief when the designer plans to sell the rights of a design or give an exclusive license for its manufacture. Income from the license or sale of a patented object may be subject only to capital gains taxes rather than as regular income. Capital gains are taxes at a maximum of half the rate of ordinary income. Obviously, this consideration applies only where the tax savings would justify the cost of patenting.